JUST UP THE ROAD

Also from Islandport Press

Moon in Full
Marpheen Chann

We're Going Home
Cynthia Thayer

Downtown, Up River
Emily Stoddard Burnham

Take it Easy
John Duncan

Whatever it Takes
May Davidson

Mountain Girl
Marilyn Moss Rockefeller

And Poison Fell From the Sky
MarieThérèse Martin

Bald Eagles, Bear Cubs, and Hermit Bill
Ron Joseph

Skiing With Henry Knox
Sam Brakeley

JUST UP THE ROAD

A Year Discovering People, Places, and What Comes Next in the Pine Tree State

chelsea diehl

Islandport Press
P.O. Box 10
Yarmouth, Maine 04096
www.islandportpress.com
info@islandportpress.com

First Edition: November 2023
Printed in the United States of America.
All photographs, unless otherwise noted, courtesy of Chelsea Diehl.

ISBN: 978-1-952143-75-5
Library of Congress Control Number: 2023946877

Dean L. Lunt | Editor-in-Chief, Publisher
Shannon M. Butler | Vice President
Emily A. Lunt | Book Designer
Author Photos by Justin Smulski

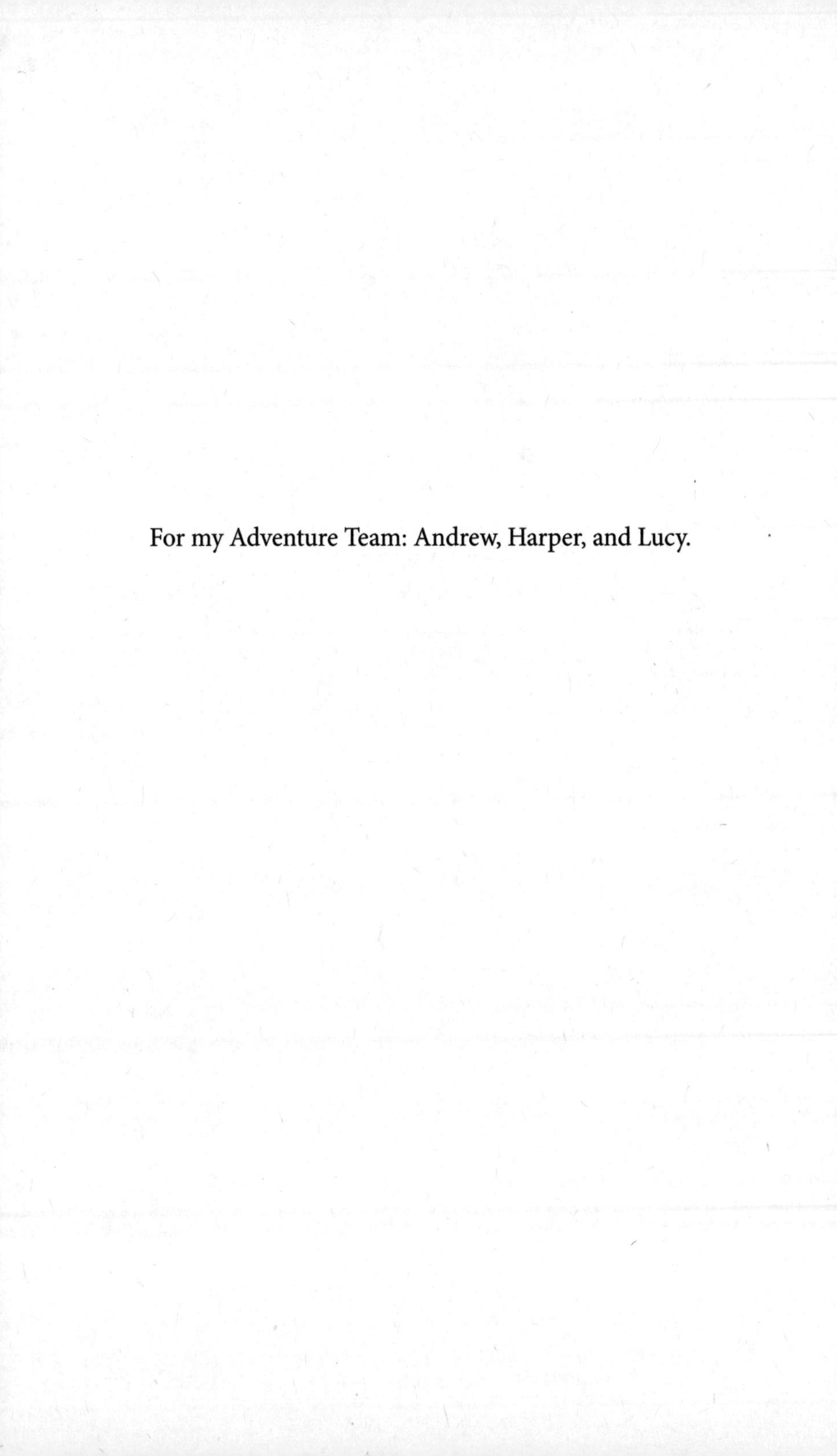

For my Adventure Team: Andrew, Harper, and Lucy.

TABLE OF CONTENTS

PROLOGUE

I left my full-time job in January 2022. Not just any job, but the only one that I had known for my entire adult life—at a company I built from the ground up with a gigantic amount of tears, joy and frustration, and an abundance of love. A company to which I was fervently devoted but where eventually the mission felt endless—a career treadmill with no defined start or end to work days. Selling my company filled me with immeasurable pride, but leaving it provided me with a previously unimaginable amount of newfound time.

So. Much. Time.

Time to figure out my second act, time to feel present with my young daughter, time to reconnect with my husband. But also time to worry. What if I left the one thing I was actually good at? Do I know how to do anything else? If I try something new, will people take me seriously as I try to reinvent myself? Who am I, really, without this job? And when did I start obsessing about what others thought of me?

I grew up in the woods in the Farmington Valley of Central Connecticut on a large pond that my grandfather maintained. Our house sat on a hill just above the pond and directly alongside the Farmington River—conveniently (for me and my siblings at least, maybe not my mom) next to a set of rapids. On lazy summer days as a teen, I'd toss my conspicuous tube into the river—a pop of pink next to the dull yellow ones rented to customers by a tubing company up the street—and ride the flow down to the company's pickup point. Soaking wet and sun kissed, carrying my somewhat deflated flamingo tube under my arm, I'd hitch a free ride back home from the bus that scooped up the waiver-signed, life-jacket-wearing tubers. The drivers never questioned me, perhaps amused by my sanguinity and how confidently I slid into line between actual customers, stuffing my pink tube on the back of the bus with the sturdy yellow ones.

"The Pond" as we affectionately called it—apparently my family was not concerned with originality— hosted every major family milestone and then some: graduation celebrations, baby showers, retirements and "just because" parties—there was a bonfire, there was food, there were feet in the sand. In high school, I'd spend all day swimming and canoeing in the treasured waters, only to hastily throw on a swim coverup to host my friends by bonfire through the evening—spending most of the night mercilessly flirting with a boy named Andrew. (Many years later at The Pond, my grandfather walked me down a makeshift sand aisle to marry Andrew.)

The majority of my childhood and young adult years were spent outdoors, lost in pretend stories I'd make up deep in the woods or writing angsty diary entries while perched high on a boulder with toes dipped in cool streams. I would be covered in bug bites, a poison ivy rash here or there, scraggly bangs hid my eyes, entirely unconcerned with how I presented myself to the world. After catching the theater bug at a performing arts camp one summer, I became absolutely enraptured with being onstage. It soon became a funny dichotomy the more serious I became about acting and all things performing arts—suddenly my summers were split between carefree sweltering beach days and memorizing lines inside air conditioned theaters. The older I got and the more deeply interwoven my life became with the arts, the less time I prioritized outdoor exploration.

My performing opportunities increased the more I trained, the more I committed to auditioning, the more I stoked the fire. By the time college rolled around, I was steadily cycling in and out of shows throughout the year, and there was nothing I wanted more on this planet than to become a professional actor. My interests were solidified, goals concrete, and I thoroughly enjoyed branding myself an actor.

I spent four years training at Emerson College in Boston. During my time at Emerson, many people—unsolicited, yet tirelessly—emphasized just how impossible it was going to be to make a living performing. In response, I began loading my schedule with theatre education classes. I was determined to prove the starving artist stereotype wrong and promised myself to put all of my being into figuring out a way to stay fulfilled—and pay my rent—from a life in the arts. My lightbulb moment arrived just before my senior year while student-teaching for Emerson's Summer Arts Academy, working with high schoolers who shared similar dreams and aspirations with my sixteen-year-old self. On the last day of camp, multiple parents approached me and asked the same thing: *could we hire you to help us prepare for college auditions?*

Loaded with false confidence, something I had continued to perfect since my tubing days, I took on my first set of private coaching clients the following summer, proudly adding "Teacher" to my invisible set of self-assigned labels.

Understanding the areas in which I fell short, I pulled together some talented friends, and we coached students on monologue, song, and dance preparation to help them tackle the highly competitive college audition process (think auditioning numbers close to three thousand for a starting freshman class of twelve at the top musical theatre programs.) The beginnings of My College Audition—a tiny company with a gigantic heart—were born.

During the next decade or so as I built the company, we moved from the Upper East Side of New York City to the North End of Boston to the Massachusetts suburbs. We welcomed our daughter, Harper, into the world, navigating the shaky ground of working parenthood, attempting to constantly perfect our juggling act. Despite our persistent inability to feel at home—this intangible discontentment that quickly followed each move, the distinct markings of temporary with every unpacked box—the one constant that always felt right to me was work. I remained consumed and infatuated, hungry to perfect systems and obsessed with SEO. My worth seemed intimately tied to the success of the business, and my value was wrapped up in my students' success. My identity, dangerously reduced, was my job title.

In 2018, we made the decision to move to Maine, tenderly referring to it as our "do-over." We had been working long hours on opposite schedules, living in a suburb where we felt completely isolated, and generally felt an overwhelming lack of connection to our surroundings. A restlessness had managed to seep into each part of our everyday lives and we knew hitting the reset button was necessary. We sold most of our belongings, rented a tiny apartment in Portland, and settled into a new place where we knew not a single person. Our couch couldn't fit through the narrow hallways of the building, so we spent our first night eating takeout on the hardwood floors of our apartment overlooking Commercial Street, watching seagulls swoop past our windows and slurping noodles while our daughter twirled about the rooms. We were swiftly struck by a welcomed, almost baffling sense of belonging. We were home.

After our move to Maine, while I continued to grow My College Audition, an opportunity arose to sell the business. Recognizing the opportunities this would provide and acknowledging that I had probably taken it as far as I could on my own, I pursued it. Relinquishing control, adopting new structures, and finally loosening my grip was, at first, torturous. But as my workload shifted, so did my understanding (even if painful) that it was time for me to try something new—the company I nurtured and grew was fully capable of thriving without me. So after two years of working for the new owners, I said goodbye to the little company I started during my senior year of college.

That's when panic set in.

I was no longer a business owner. Who was I without this badge of honor I spent years polishing? For a little girl who once proudly paraded about with dirt caked under every fingernail, it was humbling to realize how much I depended on this label—on the show, on the performance, on the validation.

I logged out of my work email for the final time on January 1, 2022, and sat down to write my New Year's resolution. Getting a job and figuring out what the heck I was doing sat at the top of the list—but I settled on something a little less formidable. I decided to take a year to give myself room to explore, to live untethered (and titleless) for a stretch of time; I would complete one hundred new adventures in Maine by year's end and hope whatever was supposed to be next for me would reveal itself along the way. I'd attempt to properly dig into the newly adopted state that I loved so much, visit every corner, give the place I aim to call my forever home my full, undivided attention. I wanted to tap back into the confidence I had enjoyed growing up, with zero regard for what others thought, knowing I'd figure it out once I got there.

With a running list of curated journeys, ones I'd been dreaming about all across the state but never had the time to pursue, I mapped out my plan for the year—making sure to leave the majority of my adventure list blank, allowing myself the joy of discovery. It was time to throw that hot pink tube back into the rapids and take off.

Just Up the Road is my love letter to Maine, written during a year when I was given the remarkable gift of time. A year when I allowed myself to live without a label, without classifying who I am, and what it is that I do. A year when I gave a warm embrace to my imposter syndrome and then promptly left it at the door. A year when I really got to know my neighbors, listened more deeply, and leaned into adventures that intimidated me. I hope these adventures, these stories from the people who know and love it most, inspire you to make the most of whatever amount of time you get to spend in this beautiful state. And if your story is in need of a revision, you give yourself the benefit of a rewrite.

Chelsea Diehl
September 2023

IN MICROSPIKES

Wood-Fired Sauna at Nurture Through Nature

Denmark, Maine

I knew I needed a resetting of sorts. A way to figuratively, and perhaps literally, shed the past ten plus years of my life to focus on the next ten. I'm all for symbolic acts that represent important change—so I decided my first adventure after leaving my job was a solo sweat session in the middle of the woods.

When you book a wood-fired sauna experience at Nurture Through Nature, a retreat center northwest of Sebago Lake, they warn you to wear appropriate walking shoes (plus traction if it's winter) and to bring a flashlight in case it's dark when you leave. With microspikes strapped on, I walked up a small hill, following wooden signs bearing encouraging messages pinned to trees, each sign providing a reminder to be present, to breathe, and to "notice." I noticed how quiet the woods were against my crunchy footsteps in the icy snow. (Seriously, was anyone else here?) I also noticed I was entirely preoccupied while trudging

The Wood Fired Sauna at Nurture Through Nature.

along the path. Relentless reminders that I was now jobless and rotating cycles of worry to exhilaration back to worry, circled endlessly in my mind. Accepting my inability to be present, I attempted to shift my focus by concentrating on my breath, watching warm exhales escape, emerging as misty clouds in the frosty air. Suddenly, the sauna appeared through the trees. A circular wood-paneled structure with a multicolored banner wrapped around the circumference was peacefully, solemnly, waiting for me.

As I approached, an employee of Nurture Through Nature emerged near the entrance, warmly welcoming me into the sauna. With enviable calmness, the woman offered snacks and water and proceeded to show me the ropes. Her voice was so soothing and deliberate and I could tell she was the type of person who is probably a pro at being "present," someone who has no problem "noticing." A relaxation professional, a mind and body easement expert, I decided. She seemed effortlessly grounded, filled with peace, clearly in touch with herself and her environment. Meanwhile, I was fully distracted again. I tuned back into my surroundings just as she sweetly asked, "Are you going to do the brook plunge?"

Behind the sauna flows a spring-fed mountain brook where guests are invited to do an icy dunk at some point during their eucalyptus-infused, steamy session. It was about five degrees outside and I couldn't feel my toes. I can't do that, I convinced myself. That's for someone else anyway, someone who has a strong connection to their emotional and physical needs, someone who is able to honor those needs. Still, I could feel this faint desire begin bubbling up from my core, a tiny voice struggling to be heard. But before I could convince my brain to follow my gut, I muffled and silenced the urge. Next time, I promised—both the voice and the tranquil employee. Next time, no matter what, I will plunge into that frigid brook. She smiled as she opened the door to exit the transition room, letting in a wash of cool air, and began her trek back down the hill.

I sat in the cedar-lined sauna on and off for one sweaty, heart-pumping hour. I took multiple breaks, feeling my heart rate climb, peeking my head out into the winter air for relief. While inside the sauna, when my ever-persistent thoughts would overwhelm me, I would take advantage of the frigid brook water provided in a large bowl and properly drench myself to be shocked back into the present. Occasionally, it worked. Perhaps it was just the pools of sweat escaping from my skin, but in a few "present" moments, I felt lighter.

When my hour wrapped and I stepped outside, my body steaming in the cold air, I was alone. I traipsed back to my car, my sweat crystallizing, and this time gave a mental high five as I passed the wooden reminders pinned to the trees.

"I'll be back," I whispered to each sign, assuring them of my vow to return.

Douglas Mountain

Baldwin, Maine

There was only a one day overlap between my last week of work and the start of my husband Andrew's new job. Just one singular day when our daughter Harper would be in school, Andrew would have an empty inbox, and I'd truly begin kicking off my new journey. Knowing we had just this one precious day together free of responsibilities (and our child) he asked me to plan a hike.

We didn't have much time before school pickup, so I chose a hike less than an hour from Portland that wouldn't take terribly long to complete. Douglas Mountain, on the western side of Sebago Lake, features short but challenging trails with a reward at the summit.

We pursued the following trail system:

The Stone Observation Tower at Douglas Mountain.

Eagle Scout Trail (1 Mile)
Nature Trail (0.7 mile loop)
Ledges Trail (0.25 miles)

At the summit, there is a Rapunzel-esque stone observation tower that offers panoramic views of Sebago Lake and a snow-capped Mount Washington in the distance. Dr. William Blackman, a New York surgeon, purchased the mountain and surrounding area in the late 1800s—eventually building the tower to share his love for the area with anyone willing to climb to the top of his cherished mountain.

After briefly pretending to be a captive princess standing atop her intricately constructed prison, I wound my way back down the tower's stone steps to return to the trail. I turned back around to see Andrew still perched in the tower, a serene smile occupying his face, resembling a prince satisfied after a successful princess rescue. He took some crisp, deep inhales while surveying his kingdom.

Once he finally descended, he grabbed my hand and said, "Let's do this."

Yes, let's, I thought. We'll tackle this next year, filled with change and a touch of fear, together. We'll support each other through shifts in schedules, new worries, joys, and everything in between. We got this.

Most likely, he was referring to the hike back to the car.

Roberts Farm Preserve

Norway, Maine

There's something special to be found in the warming hut at the 165-acre Roberts Farm Preserve, a conservation and recreation project of the Western Foothills Land Trust that features seven miles of groomed trails. Visitors are allowed to borrow cross-country ski and snowshoe equipment for free during the winter on Saturdays and Sundays. The equipment, which is plentiful and in spectacular condition, is available to anyone and everyone to try at no cost. Donations are welcome, but not required.

We are both avid downhill skiers, but Andrew and I had never tried cross-country skiing, despite a consistent longing to. Naively, I assumed the two require pretty similar skills and that we'd have no problem adjusting. How different could Nordic skiing be, after all? It's just that the toe is attached to the ski but the heel is not, yeah? However, before investing in equipment, we took advantage of the opportunity to "try before you buy" at the preserve.

With a fresh snowstorm a few days behind us, we arrived at the preserve decked out in our Maine winter finest—layers, upon layers, upon more layers. We were greeted at the warming hut by a volunteer who helped us choose the right boots, skis, and poles for our adventure. The process is seamless, well organized, and swift—and within just a few minutes, we were suited up and ready to rock.

For some reason, we had the seemingly brilliant idea to put Harper, a full-fledged kindergartener, in a snow tube and attach a harness to Andrew so he could pull her while he attempted to ski. We convinced ourselves this made a lot of sense—but to be clear, kid's snowshoes and skis are available to borrow as well. I'm not sure if we thought she'd have more fun this way, if we could get more skiing in since she wasn't skiing fully on her own yet, or what exactly—but regardless, off we went with a series of befuddled onlookers.

We headed for the easy to moderate Stephens Trail Loop. The trail, just under three miles, started off flat and we made great strides at first. I garnered a false confidence as I adjusted to the new sensation, the rise and fall of the heel, the adopted diagonal stride. Harper was indeed having fun just as we had hoped, trailing her gloved hand along the snow, making snowballs while her dad pulled her along.

However, our first hill proved a disaster of epic proportions—as did every single slope after that. While Andrew picked up a little speed—unsteadily navigating a new skiing technique—Harper's tube would race alongside of him, or sometimes shoot in front of him, causing him to awkwardly zig-zag down the hill. As Andrew tried his best to stay upright, she found it all hilarious, her laughter ricocheting through the trees. I was zero help as I struggled to find my balance, toppling hard on every hill. Once on the ground, my skis twisted and tangled, I'd wave skiers along, while muttering an awkward "I'm fine" as they attempted to help me.

It never got better. By the end of the trail I was sweating profusely and my arms and legs were quickly on their way to becoming black and blue. Andrew could barely contain himself before he was able to rip the harness off. Meanwhile, Harper was sobbing because she was so cold from lack of physical exertion in near zero temperatures.

Harper, who only recently mastered the art of sarcasm, said, "That was fun," and rolled her eyes as we pulled out of the lot. Through a fit of giggles from the backseat, we made plans to give cross-country skiing another try the following weekend—this time, we planned for everyone to pull their own weight.

Goat Hike at Ten Apple Farm

Gray, Maine

It was a balmy negative ten degrees on the day of my scheduled goat hike at Ten Apple Farm. I hopped out of the car, saw a small fire pit blazing near the barn, and beelined towards it. Soon I stood warming my hands, listening to the goats chatter from within the barn, and watching a duo of small ponies peek their heads out through the fence to get a glimpse of the stranger.

Within a few minutes, Karl, who is one-half of the husband and wife team behind the Farm, joined me at the fire pit and we struck up conversation while defrosting our fingers. We connected over stories about living in New York City, the change of life and pace that comes from living in Maine, and how lucky we are to be raising our daughters here. As he shared his family's journey to landing at the farm, I was impressed by his absolute dedication to trusting his intuition. He is a photographer while his wife, Margaret, is a writer and former manager at New York's esteemed Magnolia Bakery. After spending a year exploring the world of goats and small-scale agriculture, the duo felt inspired and ready to embrace a life of simplicity, freedom and, of course,

Philip the Sheep at the Goat Hike at Ten Apple Farm.

goats. Leaving city life behind, they landed at Ten Apple Farm in 2005. Since then they have written five books together, raised a farm full of their beloved dairy goats and various other animals, and truly live the life they imagined. This is not the course they originally charted nor the course they studied and trained for, but the one they eventually knew deep down was the right one. They weren't scared to become someone new, to shift their entire world to follow a new passion, even if at first they didn't know what the heck they were doing.

What Karl didn't know while sharing this with me was that his story was just what I needed to hear at exactly the time I needed to hear it. Deciding to take a left turn after you have established yourself in an entirely different career and lifestyle, was a decision that incessantly tugged at me for the past couple years, begging me to notice. I had created the business plan for my company only the month before graduating from Emerson College with an acting degree. I learned to build my own website, took crash courses in marketing on top of my on-camera acting classes, and became obsessively resolved to make a full life in the performing arts—no matter what. For fourteen years, I had succeeded. But now, the thing I fought and clawed for, the life and job I once loved so much, somehow left me feeling empty.

The rest of my tour group showed up—three friends from out of state visiting Maine. Judging from their attire and shoe choices, it was clear to me—and to Karl—that this might be their first time visiting Maine (in winter no less.) After inspecting the Crocs one friend had chosen for the snowy walk, Karl offered: "You want some boots?" He grabbed his personal pair from the house and the visitor gratefully threw them on. Karl then released the goats from the red barn and they came barreling down the hill. I erupted in laughter watching them bound down to us, awkwardly bumping into each other, and happily putting on a show to make their dad proud. Following the goats was Philip, a lone, plump sheep who, after years of living with his adopted goat siblings, convinced himself he was a goat as well.

Karl guided us through the woods, the goats hanging on his every command, Philip proudly parading with his family. I connected with the out-of-towners, snapped group photos with the goats and poked fun at them for being completely under-dressed. Karl answered every silly question, pointed out all of the various personalities among his herd, and educated us about the variety of things goats are used for, including dairy, fiber, and land management.

After the 1.5 mile hike was completed, we returned to the barn where Margaret waited for us with fresh goat milk and cookies. Their former garage has been repurposed into a gift store, where I snagged a "Philip Fan" shirt.

It is an inexpensive, no-brainer activity. You get some exercise, fresh air, great conversation, education, and so much more during a two-hour farm visit. And perhaps Karl and Margaret's story will inspire you, too—regardless of where you are on your journey.

Izakaya Minato

Portland, Maine

"What's your favorite restaurant in Portland?" is an impossible question. It's like trying to choose your favorite kid. But I only have one kid (she's my favorite) and if I begrudgingly had to choose *one* restaurant to bestow upon a visitor to Portland, *one* place that I think represents Portland's culinary prowess, *one* place that incorporates everything that you'd expect in Maine cuisine but with a flair and authenticity all their own—it'd be Izakaya Minato.

You'll not only leave full, jovial, and perhaps a little inspired—you will also not faint when the check comes. While it's worth every penny, luckily for all of us, the bill is always completely reasonable.

A cozy izakaya-style Japanese spot for inventive small plates on Washington Avenue, you can't go wrong with anything on the menu. However, permanent fixtures on my order list include garlic edamame, daily tempura (whatever they decide to fry up that day), shichimi tuna (seared tuna, togarashi, red onions, ponzu), JFC (Japanese Fried Chicken with spicy mayo and cabbage slaw), mochi bacon (exactly as it sounds), and the okonomiyaki (cabbage pancake with bonito). To accompany these dishes, I order a hot sake from their noteworthy list of options, and for some added fun, they let you choose your sake cup from the varying color and style options they have accumulated. The restaurant is small, bustling at all times, and just downright fun. It's impossible to not leave with your mood lifted and your belly full.

It's my favorite restaurant in Portland.

There, I said it.

Chelsea Diehl

Birch Point Beach State Park

Owls Head, Maine

My favorite season is the off-season.

I daydream about riding chairlifts up ski mountains during heat waves, watching sea smoke rise off the ocean while standing in the center of an empty, frozen-over beach. About wandering aimlessly, free of crowds, soaking up a place when it finally gets a necessary chance to recharge. About visiting a place when few others else care to.

And boy, did I visit on the polar opposite of a day most folks typically spend at Birch Point Beach State Park—a peaceful, sixty-two-acre slice of heaven not far from Owls Head in Midcoast Maine. Instead of beach blankets, thick patches of ice covered the entirety of the crescent-shaped pocket beach. No sand castle building kiddos, parents resting in the sun, or swimmers braving the chilly waters of Penobscot Bay. It was just me, traversing the frozen path in spikes and slipping occasionally while making my way to the edge of the water at this spot beloved by many locals. During the off-season, the entrance gate is closed, which adds a quarter mile of walking to reach the beach—normally a quick, easy jaunt unless you visit in the dead of winter, where each step requires heavy calculation to avoid breaking a bone.

I crunched my way to a picnic table under a few pine trees blanketed in snow. I slid my snow pants against the icy bench, resting for a moment, taking in the views. A friend told me about this beach and insisted I make the journey, although I bet they assumed I would go when the temperature stood at least in the double digits. For my friend, the kickoff to any great

Maine summer begins here—new swimsuits on, feet buried deep in the sand, and a cooler packed for a day of family hanging, beachcombing, and tide-pool searching. This was her happy place.

I looked around for other footprints in the snow, but didn't see any. I had never heard of this beach until she told me about it, and although I wasn't expecting to see anyone else here today considering the weather, I wondered how many people actually knew about this remarkable little cove. Some secrets, some cherished places, are meant to be kept close to the vest. But the ones you willingly share, knowing they might become someone else's treasured haven, can be a beautiful gift. It's not hard to fall in love with Maine, but I love when people fall in love with *my* Maine.

With extra time on my hands this year, something I am admittedly not great at dealing with, I chose to complete one hundred new adventures in Maine. I figured by the end of these adventures, some inspiration would hit me and my next steps would become clear. Maine had provided a fresh start for my family once before, after we sold next to everything we owned in Massachusetts and packed up just enough to move ourselves into a tiny apartment in Portland. We blindly followed our belief that Maine was where we were meant to raise our daughter and where we would grow old together. This was our do-over after reluctantly following what others were doing at the time—getting a house in the suburbs, commuting to work, pretending to have the newborn stage under control, and offering quick hellos while handing off the baby. All while hanging on by a thread. Moving to Maine changed our life and shocked our system—we started going outside every day, stretched ourselves socially to create a community, and loved each other harder.

Now a few years later, I hoped, one more time, to steal a little magic from Maine.

However, staring at this empty beach, a gift bestowed upon me by a trusted friend, I wondered if pursuing my own adventures through the seasons this year was actually enough of a journey. I felt I needed more of this—I needed to view Maine through other people's lenses too.

Maybe by following some shared whispers I would have an aha moment, take a bestowed adventure that would reveal the way forward and provide a welcome direction for what I should do next. At the very least, I'd meet new faces, collect inspiration from their contributions to our state, and get to see their Maine.

Perhaps, it was someone, not something, that might have the answer I was searching for.

Meet Laisee Holden

South Portland, Maine

@laisee, @lukeslobster

I live in Laisee Holden's old house. Laisee, a local Mainer with an impressive philanthropic and sports marketing resume and the ultimate wrangler of three young girls, is married to Luke Holden of Luke's Lobster. Luke's Lobster is a family-owned Maine seafood business that serves crave-worthy lobster rolls and other seafood dishes at more than thirty locations across the United States, Japan, and Taiwan.

When we stumbled upon Laisee's house, we weren't in the market to buy one, as we were still happily scrunched into our small downtown Portland apartment. But there was just something about this adorable Cape Cod nestled in our dream neighborhood near Willard Beach. Willard beach—a four-acre, small sand-and-pebble beach nestled between Fisherman's Point and the campus of Southern Maine Community College, was instrumental in our decision to move to Maine after spending a week-long vacation there.

The house incessantly occupied our thoughts for days until we decided that our year-long trial period of living in Portland was over. We were sure Maine was home and we were ready to put down roots. The day we closed on our new house, as we unbuckled our seat belts to head inside and finalize the deal, my husband placed his hand on my leg and lovingly asked, "Are you going to be weird?"

Being an actress by trade, there's not much that really rattles me. I love a big crowd, I come to life when I entertain guests, I certainly love the spotlight, and I am not easily intimidated. But my husband knows the truth. Celebrities? Not fazed. Opening night of a new show? Child's play. Being in the same room as a restaurateur? Complete buffoon.

Owning a restaurant is something that I've always secretly dreamed about. C'mon, I'm a half-decent cook and I know how to run a business, I could do it! But no, no way, I can't. A special courage surrounds these people, an unbridled fearlessness that not everyone possesses. When I attended acting school, I often heard the phrase: "if you can do anything else with your life and be happy, you should do that." I'm sure a restaurant-industry equivalent exists, and I guarantee every restaurateur—along with their immediate family—has heard it.

It's that notion, the unfettered chasing of a dream, that resonates with me and makes me jittery, awkward, thrilled. I know what it's like to attempt a life in an industry that's unforgiving and grueling. What it's like to fight for a chance to even just do your job—a job with tough hours and tricky schedules that requires you on the weekends, that comes with an understanding that you will miss friends' weddings and kids' milestones, that offers no financial security, and that is done in total service to your audience. A job that ultimately becomes a family affair with work inevitably bleeding into the everyday, requiring endless support and compassion from your significant other. You don't go into the restaurant or performing arts industry for any reason other than you have to. There's no other way.

So why do these people—whom I imagine are normal people with similar dysfunctional, hopeful dreams—make me an idiot when in their presence? I imagine it's similar to the feeling you get when you see your first Broadway play; you lose yourself in the story as soon as the lights go up.

I get swept up in the story happening behind the scenes at a restaurant. I love watching the entrances of the major characters that make up any given Friday night reservation—the chef, hostess, waitstaff. But I also wonder about the ones holding down the fort at home. Is the restaurant owned by a couple? What does their schedule look like if they have kids? What worries do they share at home after the curtain drops each night? It's the people, the creators of the production, who intrigue me most. By the time I've sat down at a new restaurant, I've already read so much, reveled in the story of how the place was built and by whom, that I've unknowingly become a groupie. In my husband's words—I get weird.

When I caught wind of who was selling this house, I was instantly transported back to the Upper East Side of New York City where my husband (then my boyfriend) and I would treat ourselves to a lobster roll at Luke's Lobster on our limited law school and actor budget. One time, while waiting in line, a customer casually pointed to the back and said to his buddy, "That's Luke"—who appeared to be knee-deep in prep work. It was the first time that feeling ran through me—like, right, someone made this place. The person in the back created this space—a place where I store date nights, memories, and daydreams about the future—it's always over food, in the beautiful comfort of a place that someone else has created for us.

But there we were at the signing for our new home. It was a beautiful Maine day. A ridiculous, picturesque, not-a-cloud-in-the-sky day. We were laughing with our realtor. I pretended to be calm.

Suddenly, in walked the Holdens. On all accounts, they were extremely normal, supremely nice; just two Mainers happy to hand over some keys. I was a bubbly mess.

Laisee, who was saying goodbye to the house where she first brought home her oldest daughter, was kind, calm, and interested in getting to know us. She is proud to be Luke's Lobster's number one fan, and although I've never asked and she'd probably never say so, I imagine her support from the sidelines, just off backstage, is integral to the story and growth of Luke's Lobster.

After getting to know Laisee more, she remains humble, gracious, and generous—she is a Mainer after all. And she knows better than anyone, after growing up and raising her daughters here, that in Maine you get to know your neighbor—even if that neighbor is me and she happens to be a little much.

Maine in Laisee's Words

A Favorite Maine Adventure

"When in Maine, there is nothing better than getting out on the water and lobstering. Hauling lobster traps is a unique and memorable experience. Our daughters love to check what surprises crawl in each trap; it's like a treasure hunt for them. Rocky Bottom Fisheries on Portland Pier is a great way to experience the life of a lobsterman and enjoy a hands-on demonstration tour."

Last Meal on Earth Somewhere in Maine

"I'm very biased, but I would say a lobster roll at Luke's Lobster. There's nothing more 'Maine' than eating lobster out on their deck on the ocean, watching the commercial boats come in with their catch and drop it at the nearby buying station. I love that Luke's Lobster highlights each part of the ocean-to-plate process."

A Person in Maine You Admire

"I worked for Peter Carlisle, the head of Olympics and Action Sports at Octagon Sports Agency, for ten years. I admire everything about Peter, especially the fact that he invested himself and his business in the state of Maine. Even as his company changed and grew, Peter insisted on remaining in Maine. From his base in Portland he has represented famous Olympians Michael Phelps, Simone Biles, Ross Powers, Aly Raisman, and many other exceptional athletes. Peter has put Maine on the map in the sports marketing world.

Many, like myself, have come to Maine for the chance to work with Peter Carlisle. From Peter I learned that a confident, creative person can forge their own path and become highly successful. Peter also taught me the importance of having a good work-life balance. Peter Carlisle is the smartest person I know. It is no wonder he chose to live in Maine."

Why You Call Maine Home

"Maine is a special place to call home. I feel incredibly lucky to be raising my three daughters in such a close-knit community. It's fun to see them enjoying exploring the coast, just as I did as a kid. I grew up in Cape Elizabeth and was thrilled to get the opportunity to move back to Maine later in life. Home should be where you're happiest, where you're supported, where you learn and grow, where you're surrounded by grounded and hard-working people, and where people prioritize our environment . . . and for me, that's Maine."

Luke's Lobster, Portland Pier

Portland, Maine

Andrew and I have been on a secret crusade to convince his parents to move to Maine. When we moved to Portland, we did not know a single person. We were confident, and it's since proven true, that we would find our people and create a chosen family of our own—but still, there's no replacement for having family close. We've taken my in-laws up and down the Maine coast, showed them our wildest finds, secret gems, and most stunning hikes with sweeping summits. We've introduced them to restaurants across the state, often overwhelming them with the endless dinner possibilities on any given evening.

The first place we took them in our Move to Maine propaganda campaign was lunch at Luke's Lobster off Commercial Street. Tucked into a spacious interior against a wall of windows overlooking Portland's working waterfront, my in-laws were, justifiably, distracted by the views. Seal heads popped up around the pier, fire pits roared on the deck, and lobster boats returned with their hauls. By the end of their fried haddock bites and lobster rolls, I knew the initial hooks were set. Andrew and I exchanged sneaky smiles between bites of our crab rolls.

Since that first meal, my in-laws always have lunch at Luke's, with or without us in tow, when they visit Maine. It's become their happy place and they return from lunch dates smiling, full, and imagining what life could be like in Portland. Will they move to Maine? The verdict is still out—so, in the meantime, we'll continue our mission by devouring fresh lobster rolls with them at Luke's.

Blueberry Mountain & Rattlesnake Flume and Pool

Stow, Maine

I'm a mosquito magnet.

If you want to enjoy the outdoors and remain free of bug bites, stand next to me. I will attract any gnat within a one-mile radius and magically develop gigantic, itchy welts immediately following every bite. I persevere because, well, I love being outside and that's just nature—although I can definitely be a little bit (or a lot of bit) dramatic when I'm being swarmed by bugs.

I extensively researched this hike, located in Evan's Notch, which is part of White Mountains National Forest in Western Maine. Some portions of the trail sit on private property, generously made available for others to enjoy. I read about people's experiences plucking and enjoying blueberries along the trail, the stunning views of Shell Pond and neighboring mountains from the summit, and what seems to be everyone's favorite reward at the end of the hike—the crystal clear, turquoise-colored swimming hole and waterfall, Rattlesnake Pool and Flume. I also read that during the summer months it gets pretty crowded with people . . . and mosquitoes. Both of these things are, of course, not surprising but I created a vivid, unshakable image of being mauled by swarms of bugs while crowds of people hovered around and gawked over me. Did I mention that I am an actress?

So, after blowing these obstacles completely out of proportion, I decided to avoid them altogether. I'd hike during winter, although I also knew I'd have to suck it up and come back to explore this beauty during the summer months to actually swim in the pool. Little did I know, battling mosquitoes would have been a micro-problem compared to what I actually faced during my off-season hike.

I left home before sunrise. As I neared the New Hampshire and Maine border, it became clear I'd underestimated how much snow remained on the ground in Western Maine. Not deterred (I packed appropriately for the hike), I continued to follow my GPS.

Trusting my gut, not my GPS, is a lesson I must constantly relearn. As I began making my way to the trailhead I had typed in, the road suddenly became considerably more slick and difficult. At first, I thought my car would be fine so I cautiously continued following the route. But as I inched along, I eventually entertained the idea this route was unsafe, and that it was time to turn off the GPS. I had only driven a few feet from the gravel road, so I threw the car in reverse, pressed the gas, and, somehow, immediately, backed directly into a snowbank.

Crap. I was stuck. Like, really stuck. I tried digging myself out (using mostly my gloved hands) to no avail. After repeated attempts to free myself, I reluctantly decided to call someone for help. Of course, as I quickly discovered, I had no cell service. The closest house was a ways away—so back to digging out the car I went. After an hour, and a couple busted knuckles, I gave up. I grabbed my pack to start making my way to find help.

As I slammed the door to begin my walk of shame, a miracle appeared in the form of a blue Subaru. I frantically waved to the car as it pulled alongside the gravel road to park (because they knew, obviously, not to attempt driving on the road I was on in the winter). I waited to greet the lucky person who happened to drive right into this panic zone. Suddenly, three doors swung open and (this is my husband's least favorite part of the story) three extremely tall and seemingly strong men piled out of the car to my rescue. Decked out in hiking gear, they immediately got to work digging the car out of the snow. While I piled them with apologies and endless thank yous, they pushed the car out, reversed it to a safe spot and saved my day—in just two minutes.

I started to cry out of pure relief (again, I'm dramatic) and through my muffled tears I begged them to allow me to Venmo them money to pay for a round of drinks after their hike. They refused and promised me it was no big deal. As they began to disappear down the trail, one of my saviors turned around and with a warm smile said, "Hey, it's still a beautiful day for a hike. Don't let this get you down—get out there!"

Resolved to just get back home, I brushed this off and slumped back into my car. I was embarrassed, angry with myself for letting this happen and frustrated to have driven so far only to completely waste a gorgeous day. As I sat feeling sorry for myself, the sun peeked out from around the clouds and lit up the forest, welcoming me despite my mistake. After a few exhales to collect myself, I grabbed my gear and headed to the mountain.

It was a challenging hike given the amount of snow on the ground. I was exhausted after my animated morning, so I ventured only to the Rattlesnake Pool to complete a two-mile out and back adventure (see, look at me, listening to my gut!) Even while shrouded in snow, the pool was a crisp, stunning emerald blue and I was proud of myself for making the most of the day after a chaotic start. I kept looking for the Subaru Saviors, but I never saw them again, nor did I see one other person that day.

On my next trip to Blueberry Mountain, it will be a warm, muggy, weekend day filled with lots of people sharing the trail. I'll drive up to the trailhead safely, confidently. I'll be sprayed head to toe in bug spray and will finally complete the following four-ish mile loop:

Up White Cairn Trail
Down Stone House Trail
Pitstop at Rattlesnake Pool off of Stone House Trail

I'll swim in the pool, soothe the inevitable mosquito welts, and feel grateful that I get to enjoy Maine's beauty in all seasons—even if, occasionally, I might need the help and kindness of strangers to do so.

Black Mountain of Maine

Rumford, Maine

"I know you from somewhere. How do I know you, honey?" asked the sweet, older woman behind the bar as she slid an Allagash White my way. I laughed, only because minutes before someone in the café also said I looked really familiar. Did I shoot a commercial for this ski mountain back during my peak performing days that I forgot about? Or were these just friendly Mainers who strike up convo with so many people daily that eventually they'll encounter après-ski doppelgangers? After racking my brain for a bit, it was definitely the latter.

I seem to forget every year, or mentally block it out, just how expensive skiing is. Also, between getting the gear on and off (for both you and potentially your children), warming up, riding the lift, getting lunch, etc. you forget how little skiing you actually do in a day. Between the price tag and so little time spent on skis, I often drag my feet when it comes to making ski-trip plans.

But after visiting Black Mountain, located in Maine's western mountains, I honestly am not sure I will consistently go anywhere else besides here. It is relatively inexpensive, accessible, and friendly. Harper attended a two-hour children's group lesson but she essentially ended up having a private lesson. She was already riding the chairlift and skiing down the mountain by herself for the first time by the time we picked her up. You can actually ski here. Intense lines don't form at the chair lifts, which allows for a quick and easy trip to the top, while on the descent down the mountain you don't have to play dodgeball for the entirety. There is so much room to breathe and you'll find, like I did, that you're often the only person on a trail. I packed in more runs during my two-hour kid-free window than I do sometimes in a full day at other mountains.

This mountain, from the slopes to the staff to the Last Run Pub and Café, is free of pretension. It's a mountain that doesn't take itself too seriously, and in turn, you are able to focus on what skiing should be about without draining your wallet. For me, that's spending time with my family outside, getting some exercise, creating memories, and, most importantly, rewarding myself with a beer at the end of the day and striking up conversation with the bartenders. It's somewhere that everyone knows your name—or at least they think they do.

Meet Carla Tracy

South Portland, Maine

@carla_tracy

There's a common thread when I look at any of my itineraries. My hours of meticulous research, secured dinner reservations, and careful selections of stays always end up revealing a prevailing theme. And that theme is Carla Tracy.

Carla Tracy is a travel, food, and drink publicist who serves as the public-relations person for some of the most celebrated places in Maine; places that often hold the top spots on my must-try list and produce experiences that become some of my most treasured family memories. It's not a coincidence that Carla's list of clients weave in and out of my travel plans—it's a direct result of her being good at her job. She's good at her job because she's not just pitching about Maine, she's fervently experiencing and deeply immersing herself here—so the awareness she creates around her clients and the buzz circling their endeavors is authentic and justified. You trust the buzz because you know it's being generated by someone who is active in their community, someone who has thoroughly scoped out the scene.

I swear she is everywhere. Carla is probably sitting next to you at that new restaurant opening, and she definitely has tickets to that event that sold out months ago. You may have just passed her while walking on a trail in Acadia National Park or floated by her on a kayak heading to one of the Casco Bay islands. She may have just grabbed the last scone at that hidden gem of a bakery for breakfast, and you may see her again at happy hour at the new hotel bar.

If she's listed as the public-relations contact on a website, you know it's a place she doesn't just want the public to fall in love with, but one she's head over heels in love with herself.

I often wonder if my seemingly quenchless need to explore Maine is going to fade one day. If someday I will no longer feel the desire to almost exclusively travel within my own state. I still wake up each day almost pinching myself that, even when other things in my life feel chaotic or unbalanced, I have Maine. And maybe that's what unknowingly draws me to Carla and her recommendations—we both feel like we are just scratching the surface. Her enthusiasm for all things local is contagious, and she provides a daily reminder to love where you live, to never stop digging in, to ferociously celebrate and foster your community. She deeply loves Maine, and she's going to do her best to make sure you do too.

....

Maine in Carla's Words

A Favorite Maine Adventure

"As someone who is obsessed with traveling this state, this is incredibly difficult to answer but my mind first goes to a place that we frequent not only because of proximity to where we live but because of all the wonderful weekends and vacations we've spent in the area surrounding Waldoboro, Maine. I think that in Maine especially, when you can find a place that intersects the woods with water, you'll find some very special nature experiences and exceptionally good food, drink, and creative community. We love to base camp at Tops'l Farm and a perfect weekend includes oysters at Glidden Point, pizza and beer at Odd Alewives, a trip to Bristol when the actual alewives are running up the ladder, and a charcuterie and exceptional veggie plate at Broad Arrow Farm. Plus some hikes or a canoe down the Medomak River to burn those calories. Seeing seals from a canoe in the Medomak River when the tides change is a real treat! Back to Tops'l Farm for some fireside s'mores and stories, a good glass of wine, and the sound of silence."

Last Meal on Earth Somewhere in Maine

"Spicy night market soup at Long Grain in Camden, Maine. If you've had it, you know. I can't name another single dish that wanders into my head without warning (well wait, the lobster casoncelli at Aragosta in Deer Isle just did because the sauce alone will take you to another place)."

A Person in Maine You Admire

"Adam Shepherd, who is the Executive Director of Rippleffect. Rippleffect is a nonprofit in Portland that promotes youth development and leadership through adventure, healthy communities, and sustainable living. The skills and experiences in nature—woods, water, and more—that they offer to Portland's youth are truly remarkable and life-changing for some. And their commitment to diversity, equity, and inclusion creates a safe and welcoming environment for all. When my own son was old enough for their summer camp program (3rd grade), even one week with Rippleffect made a profound and lasting impression on him."

Why You Call Maine Home

"There's a saying, 'I'm not from Maine, but I got here as fast as I could.' I call Maine home, ultimately, because I'm raising my family here. There were small steps that got me here: vacations with family in York, Maine, when I was growing up. My Italian grandfather immigrated to Portsmouth, New Hampshire, with his parents and eight siblings when he was five and subsequently had relatives own and operate the old York Beach Motel and Cottages. I met friends from Maine when I went to college in upstate New York. I met my husband skiing at Sugarloaf Mountain because I was visiting one of my college friends here. Even before we had kids, it was a calculated choice to move to Maine (my side of the family lives in the Mid-Atlantic) and the community of friends and other family we have here have made it worth it a million times over. Maine was home before I ever called it that."

....

Long Grain

Camden, Maine

It's absolutely my responsibility to continue to pass this on—you must try the spicy night market noodle soup at Long Grain, an intimate restaurant on Washington Street in Camden that dishes up Thai fare. I would have never ordered this on my own without Carla Tracy's recommendation and, frankly, I am really not a soup gal. But this bowl of hot-sweet-sour broth, rice noodles, roasted Maine farm pork, bean sprouts, peanuts, and pork rinds have made me a convert.

I had gotten takeout from Long Grain in years past, but finally, upon their reopening of in-person dining after COVID, I was able to sit inside for the first time. After a full morning of hiking, I cozied up to the bar and slurped my way through the entire bowl. Their takeout is always fantastic, but this dish, as I learned, can only be fully appreciated by enjoying a freshly prepared, steaming-hot bowl served within their own walls.

And now, bestowed with this gift of knowledge, it's your responsibility to tell a trusted friend about the best soup in Maine.

Wiggly Bridge to York Harbor Cliff Walk

York, Maine

Early March can be tough in Maine. The days are short, and darkness continues to creep in well before dinner time. It's still very much winter and the weather is wildly unpredictable. When you wake up each morning you could be greeted with rain, a semi-promising warm day, or a full-fledged snowstorm.

I started the year off as if shot from a cannon. I was an adventure-seeking fiend planning and pursuing multiple trips every week, sometimes even a handful in just one day. But as March crept in, I felt my pace slowing. Maybe part of the initial thrill of enjoying Zoom-meeting-free days was wearing off. Or perhaps I was starting to see these Maine adventures as mere

Wiggly Bridge in York, Maine.

distractions when instead I should be focusing on my next steps in life. Or maybe I was just totally, completely fatigued by the idea of yet again piling on endless insulated layers just to head outside for the day. However, on this day, as I reluctantly zipped up my fleece-lined windbreaker and cursed the cold temperature outside, I again felt the familiar buzz of anticipation as I headed out the door. So, with gratitude back in place, I headed to Wiggly Bridge in York.

Wiggly Bridge, just seventy-five feet in length, is considered the world's smallest suspension bridge and is limited to foot traffic. At the end you'll find Steedman Woods, which hosts a short, scenic half-mile trail. After enjoying a little wiggle on the bridge and a stroll through the woods, I noticed a sign for the Fisherman's Walk across the street and decided to extend my journey. Warmed up, I walked along the water, stopping to admire the historic homes and boats dotting the edge of the trail, until I arrived at York Harbor Beach. I walked along the tiny beach and watched dogs jump in and out of the small waves when I bumped directly into another trail—the York Harbor Cliff Walk. Exactly as it sounds, it's a stroll along the shore with excellent views of the beach and beyond.

I'd suggest the exact out-and-back route I stumbled upon:

Wiggly Bridge, Steedman Woods and
Fisherman's Walk (1.7 miles)
York Harbor Cliff Walk (1 mile)

The sun emerged as I completed the series of unplanned trails, and, as if to say "I told you so," the rays made it warm enough to remove a layer.

IN BEAN BOOTS

Porter Preserve

Trevett, Maine

What am I doing? This was the only question that dominated my thoughts while I drove ninety minutes to the Boothbay Harbor area on an early spring afternoon (otherwise known as mud season in Maine). It was a Tuesday morning, and, on a normal Tuesday before I left my job, I would have spent the day in a series of meetings followed by back-to-back private coaching lessons during the evening. Joining forces with the company that acquired my business had been a serious adjustment. We operated on entirely different schedules; theirs was a typical 9-to-5 workday, while mine primarily featured evenings and weekends. I attempted to make both schedules work, saying yes to every opportunity and meeting invite; diving head first into the trap of busyness. I wanted our new relationship to not only work, but to thrive. And if I am being honest, I also felt a sick satisfaction from never having a moment to myself. I worked

Porter Preserve in Trevett, Maine.

with the new team for two years after the acquisition—and in a way, those years flew by, along with my life outside of work.

During that time, making a three-hour round-trip drive to the Midcoast to take a small hike was certainly never on a Tuesday docket. And now, I was questioning how it managed to get on the schedule for today. The trip felt unfounded, wrong and a massive waste of time. My goal to complete these one hundred adventures in a year was fully self imposed—but with each passing day, I struggled with why I had made this decision. In addition to filling all my newfound time (old habits die hard), I wasn't sure what I hoped to find by the end of this effort anymore. Was it enlightenment? Was it a job? I had blindly put my faith in the idea that Maine would reveal to me my next steps. Perhaps today, despite my doubts, I would find the answer nestled along a trail in the woods.

I still felt pretty defeated—and silly—as I parked at the trailhead. I was too busy brooding to notice I was the only person on the trail, and mine was the lone car in the parking lot. Simple things like this, moments of peace and solitude, were gifts I would have killed for just a few months earlier. And now I was just letting them pass me by.

Luckily for me, I picked the right trail to soothe a wandering, distant mind. This short 1.1-mile loop trail is easy, and if you hike the loop straight through, it's only about a twenty-minute walk. However, I can't imagine many people actually complete the trail that quickly. Old spruce, oak, and pine trees shade the trail, and around almost every bend, there is a scenic overlook coupled with inviting benches surveying small, rocky beaches along the Sheepscot River—all begging to be explored. Each vista was more impressive than the one before it, and just as I would put my camera lens cap back on, I'd find a new spot that needed its attention. It went on like this for two hours before I finally completed the loop.

As I do after every new adventure, I added the trail, the date completed, and a handful of observations to the adventure list that I keep on my phone. For what reason, other than to hold myself accountable, I'm not sure. And while the answer to my earlier questions wasn't hiding in the trees along this trail, I did leave the parking lot more confident that I was, eventually, going to find it.

Meet Blake Hayes

Kittery Point, Maine
@blakehayes

One of the first people I got to know after moving to Maine was Blake Hayes. Although I should clarify here—up until this year, I had never actually spoken to Blake.

On our way to preschool drop-off each morning, I turned on *The Blake Show* on Coast 93.1. Harper pointed out new buildings she noticed on the drive, we talked about which new playground we'd visit after school, and I laughed listening to Blake play games with listeners who called his radio show. His voice accompanied our drives, and, like thousands of others in Maine, I felt like I knew him. There was a comfort, a welcomed consistency, in hearing something familiar each day while we explored our new terrain.

The irony is that Blake and I should have met years prior. We both attended Emerson College, graduating only a year apart. Our dorms were one block from each other, we have tons of mutual friends, and Emerson's undergraduate enrollment is less than four thousand. We likely sat next to each other in the dining hall, scoured the same shelves in the library, and maybe, at some point, had a crush on the same guy. We both moved to New York City after graduation, and stuffed our dreams inside tiny, overpriced city apartments; we were determined to make it work. As I often joke about Emerson, no one goes there without knowing what they want to be when they grow up. Blake and I were no different.

About six months after we moved to Maine, the first car Andrew and I purchased together as a couple finally ran its course. Our new vehicle came with a six-month trial subscription to satellite radio. During that period, just as Maine began to slowly feel like home, my mornings listening to Blake on local radio were replaced by 90s tunes, some Pop2K, and a sprinkling of the Classic Rewind channel.

By the time we were approaching our one-year anniversary, we'd made new friends, fallen in love with our new community, and eaten too much seafood; we felt, finally, like we belonged. One rainy May morning after the satellite radio subscription expired, I pressed the FM button and turned on Coast 93.1 again, excited to pick up again with Blake. I remember pulling into a parking spot outside my gym listening to Blake's voice for the first time in months. Something was noticeably different—his voice was heavy and raw, his pace significantly slower. I heard an unmistakable heartache in his voice that was palpable and new. He wasn't where I had left him. At some point while I was listening elsewhere, Blake's whole world had stopped.

I skipped the gym that day and sat inside my car, learning of the sudden passing of Blake's partner, Kyle. After taking some time away from work, Blake was back behind his mic, a place where he had spent the majority of his life. He was grieving. My heart sank during his long pauses, those moments when he couldn't distract himself and when his pain seeped through. No one ever knows what to say when there is a loss. Most people turn inward, choosing silence—but by virtue of his job and his devotion to his listeners, Blake was doing all of the talking. There's something beautifully therapeutic, and heartwrenching, about no one talking back.

As I started listening again, there were days he felt okay and days when the darkness crept in. His listeners, an estimated one hundred thousand, found the same solace in Blake they always had, but this time, their comfort was in hearing him say he was all right. They tuned in day after day to make sure his pauses got shorter.

And just as time marches onward, time also heals. Today, years later, in between recaps of his weekend adventures and the morning's hot topics, I've listened as Blake found peace, fell in love, got married, and became a stepdad—all shared from the comfort of his studio, behind his mic, at the same time every weekday. He's a bright, funny, charismatic constant in so many people's lives.

Before I met Blake this year, I wondered what he'd be like in person. In his field, there's an element of showbiz and of playing the part you are assigned. It becomes easy, speaking from my experience as an actor, to shield what's really happening underneath the cloak of the character you play. You give just enough, but not everything. And sometimes when you step offstage, or go off air, the lines between reality and work become blurred. It's hard to know what's real and what's not, and what's actually me and what's my role. Do I really feel this way or, in an effort to safeguard, is this the way I need to present to people how I feel? You can become a master of your own strategic, confusing story.

But Blake is Blake. In a way that is both admirable and impressive, he gives listeners his wholly raw self. He's let Maine in like a trusted best friend. With an army of fans tuning in while the world continues to spin, he isn't afraid to share both the good and the heartbreaking without any armor. A welcomed reminder of the power of authenticity from the very first person I "met" in Maine.

Maine in Blake's Words

A Favorite Maine Adventure

"One of the things that I love about living in Kittery, is that to take the dogs for a walk off leash and get a quick thirty-minute loop in, there are so many options. Are these trails that I would tell someone to do who is only spending limited time in Maine? No, but there is something so magical about hiking in the woods, right next to the water. Like Winnick Woods in Cape Elizabeth, Rogers Park in Kittery, Wiggly Bridge in York. There are so many places you can disconnect in Maine without having to go far.

"One of my absolute favorites is Littlejohn Island Preserve in Yarmouth. The fact that it is only four spaces makes it feel remote and you aren't going to see a ton of people. That was where I went on my first date with my now husband, Tim. Can I say that we fell in love there? Probably.

"I made the mistake once of saying 'a hike is just a walk in the woods.' And anytime my friends would do a hike, like Katahdin or something, they would say, 'Just a walk in the woods, right, Blake?' And I was like, OK, I shouldn't have said it. But then Kyle got me into hiking because he loved it. He loved the isolation of it. I hiked with him, not real big hikes, nothing crazy—but after he died, I thought, there's something about hiking that connects you to people you have lost, to yourself, to strangers. I found that, for me, hiking after Kyle died was a huge part of that grieving process. There is so much power in standing somewhere that you knew someone else stood. Walking a trail that I knew he had walked but I had never done with him—because it felt like we could do it together. Trees that you pass that are older than anyone you miss—and they are still there. So life does go on, things continue to move forward and grow."

Last Meal on Earth Somewhere in Maine

"If I had to choose one last meal—it's not just the ingredients, it's the place where you are, the way that you feel when you eat, and the people you are surrounded by, it would be The Lost Kitchen. It was an experience I had with Kyle, who was not a terribly adventurous eater. There we were at a place where you don't know what the menu will be, and still, he ate everything. The second time I went, we were supposed to go back with Kyle. He had passed a few weeks before. And the way that meal felt . . . There is something about driving two hours down a dirt road, past the lonely post office, to a mill, buying the wine beforehand because it's a dry town—it creates a destination.

"But! If I could construct a final meal—I would have: a squash-blossom salad from Primo Restaurant in Rockland to start; chips, salsa and margaritas from XYZ in Southwest Harbor; a mojito from Havana in Bar Harbor; an uni spoon from Izakaya Minato in Portland; the sole Francaise from Street and Company in Portland; and dessert would be anything that Ilma Lopez from Chaval in Portland makes. Oh, and a dessert cocktail from the Wallingford Dram in Kittery."

A Person in Maine You Admire

"Erin French of The Lost Kitchen. She could open restaurants anywhere—and instead she makes her hometown better. I love that."

Why You Call Maine Home

"I love that I can access an incredible restaurant, go to a beach, hike a mountain, all while feeling safe and welcomed. Maine has a mutual love and respect for its space and its people. When you ask other people what they love about Maine, it's usually easy for them to rattle off a few things—but there is always something they can't articulate. And maybe that's the secret. Maybe what we love about Maine is something we can't articulate."

Littlejohn Island Preserve

Yarmouth, Maine

Part of the thrill of this trail resides in whether or not you will actually get to pursue it. With only four parking spots at the trailhead in Yarmouth, it's hit or miss on any given day. And if you park illegally, idle, or try to squeeze your car in on the shoulders—chances are you will be towed. You can park farther away somewhere else on Littlejohn Island (Cousins Street, along the Cousins Island Bridge, or the Cousins Island side of the Littlejohn Causeway) but that will extend your trip significantly, turning this 1.3-mile loop trail into 3.5 miles or more.

A glutton for punishment, I will only pursue the trail if I am able to snag one of the four spots. It's part of the experience for me. I'm buzzing with anticipation as I make my way over Cousins Island Bridge, anxious as I drive the strict 15-mph speed limit over Pemasong Lane, and then hold my breath as I get my first glimpse of the parking lot. To give some perspective, I've attempted to tackle this trail a dozen times—and have successfully completed it three times.

But oh, this trail, this sweet oasis. You know that you'll be only one of four car loads here (plus any surrounding neighbors) so you'll have the place (almost) to yourself. At low tide, which luckily coincided with nabbing a parking spot, handfuls of little pocket beaches reveal themselves along the edge of the trail. Tide pools filled with all sorts of creatures appear. Bald eagles and great horned owls also often nest here—I mean, if I was a majestic bird, I'd like to think that I would choose this spot to start my family as well.

If you are doing this trail correctly, in my opinion, it should take you quite a bit of time to complete what is otherwise a short loop. Give into the temptation to stop and explore every nook and cranny and allow more time than you think you need for this little adventure. Even better, bring a book, find an oak tree to relax against, and stay until sunset to watch the colors change over Casco Bay.

Snug Harbor Farm

Kennebunk, Maine

"I'll go in for just one small succulent," she said. "I'll head to Greenhouse #3, keep my eyes down, and just leave with the one present I need," she repeated to herself.

On the way to the designated greenhouse, eyes on the prize, she can't help but notice a gorgeous stone owl that her husband would just love. And what's a stone owl without a carved friend to join him in the front yard? And even though she knows not to set foot into the tropical jungle that is Greenhouse #2, an irresistible force pulls her into the humid, rare-plant playground. She emerges from the lush sanctuary, drunk from the possibilities of turning her own home into a plant paradise and somehow has another item tucked under her arm.

As she passes the chickens in their coop and the bunny barn, she stumbles to the register with a topiary, an owl, and his frog friend, a Snug Harbor signature terra cotta pot, one candle, and a plant she can't name. Success, she thinks, as she drives away without the succulent she went in for.

If you can visit Snug Harbor Farm, an immersive property in southern Maine filled to the brim with rare plants, and leave with the one item you went in for—I bow down to you. Between exploring the four deliberate, thoughtful greenhouses, each stocked with its own plant specimens, visiting the animals, and being wide-eyed in the barn filled to the brim with things you didn't know you needed, your willpower is sure to be tested.

Cascade Falls

Saco, Maine

"Let's just do whatever's easiest!" This is, unequivocally, one of my least favorite sentences. Because—*why?* Why not put effort into planning to make sure you make the most of every single day? Every moment? Every opportunity? Sometimes the greatest experiences require detailed planning—hours of research and hard work. I also shiver when I hear, "Let's just go with the flow!" for the same reasons, but even worse—because the idea of no plan whatsoever is infinitely more terrifying to me than at least having an "easy" one.

I don't want to travel to a place with no plan only to later learn I missed a once-in-a-lifetime experience only a few yards away. I don't want to plop down tons of money on a nice meal without trying the dish the restaurant is best known for or worse risk not being able to eat there at all because I didn't make a reservation. I look at my calendar each month and pre-plan my "spontaneous" days—a couple of nights I keep free to *plan* to be *spontaneous*. My sister still makes fun of me for a trip to Italy we took a few years ago—I mapped out every fifteen minutes including restroom breaks and potential cat naps on a detailed, color-coordinated Google doc. I am, admittedly, intense.

My aversion to being carefree can undoubtedly hold me back. I'm always mentally onto the next thing even when I'm physically at the place I planned to be. But being rigid—and very stubborn—works to my advantage most of the time in regards to planning, until it doesn't. When plans fall through, a reservation gets canceled unexpectedly, someone is sick, or the day doesn't follow my schedule, I unravel completely. My heart rate quickens, and my face and ears turn bright red. You'd best avoid me.

The day didn't go as planned when I first set out to visit Cascade Falls, just off Route 98 on the southern Maine coast not far from Old Orchard Beach. I had attempted to visit in February on a bitter cold morning, hoping to see a frozen waterfall. When I opened the car door to an icy parking lot, I reached for my microspikes that I always leave on the passenger floor only to find I left them in my hiking bag, which was nice and toasty back in my warm house. I felt my ears flush.

But this hike was my plan for the day, so I was going to get to that waterfall. The loop trail is only a half-mile long, which at a normal speed, should take about ten minutes. It's an easy stroll to start your day, offers plenty of time to enjoy the waterfall, and takes minimal effort. But not on a day like today.

I threw my camera over my shoulder, carefully stepped into the slippery parking lot, and immediately fell. I managed to shield my camera, but the right side of my body was another story. I got up, shook it off, took a deep breath, and slithered to the trail. I pushed my way to the small hill that brings you down to the waterfall. I gripped the wooden railing just before the descent and assessed how I could possibly get down that hill. Just as I landed on a strategy of equal parts butt scooting and desperately gripping tree branches, I fell again. Hard. This time my camera wasn't shielded.

I furiously slid my way to a tree to lean against and assess the damage (and impending bruises). Miraculously, my camera was still okay, some scratches on the body, but nothing detrimental. My body, however, was throbbing in pain, aching through my snow pants. How many more falls would it take for me to jump ship? Eventually, I very reluctantly abandoned my plan to see a

Cascade Falls in Saco, Maine.

frozen waterfall. I (literally) crawled back to my car with my tail between my legs.

I realized as spring wore on, I had been focused so intently on the ending of my journey, on what the finale will be, that I had become entirely unwilling to stray from my schedule. I have been so furiously trying to complete my adventures and finding satisfaction in checking off boxes on my list that I am rushing to the finish line and probably missing *it* entirely. I'm not listening while the music is playing, I'm just anticipating the next song in the shuffle. Always being ten steps ahead doesn't lend itself well to being present.

I've got to chill out. If anything this year, I can work on breathing some spontaneity into my daily life to help shift my focus from always driving towards resolution, to trying to find happiness in the process. Perhaps even, once in a while, I should attempt to "go with the flow." Cringe.

A few months after the aborted winter visit to Cascade Falls, I was in Southern Maine trying out a new breakfast spot. It was an unseasonably warm early Spring day, icicles dripping to their ends on buildings. I passed Cascade Falls and continued to drive for a bit, but in a sudden, uncharacteristic move, I made a U-turn. This time, with ice cleared from the parking spot and with signs of spring peeking out from the trailhead, I not only completed the trail, but also ended up doing it three times, lingering at the waterfall with each loop.

It turns out, early spring is the perfect time to visit this waterfall because the parking lot is empty of summer folks but, with snowmelt, the waterfall gorgeously rushes, cascading and crashing into a pool. An unplanned gift from an unexpected warm day, forcing the waterfall to just go with the flow.

Noted, universe. Noted.

Langlais Sculpture Preserve

Cushing, Maine

It's not every day you encounter a satirical structure of Richard Nixon sitting in a marshy pond on your morning stroll. But that you will—along with sixty-five other quirky, whimsical, massive wooden structures at the Langlais Sculpture Preserve, a sculpture and nature preserve in Midcoast Maine at the former homestead of artist Bernard Langlais. A Maine native, Langlais studied and worked in New York in the 1950s and developed a modernist painting style filled with big, bold colors and flattened perspectives. In the mid-1960s, after calling it quits in New York, he cultivated a love of working with scraps of wood and built captivating wood sculptures on the land surrounding his Cushing home.

The loop to enjoy the pieces is under half a mile, but I was delighted to discover an additional half-mile trail through the wooded portion of the property allowing you to take a full mile stroll to not only enjoy the art, but the natural beauty of the Cushing peninsula as well. Additionally, the trail is ADA accessible and free with plenty of parking. Accessible art for all, my friends.

The first time I visited, I was the only person on the trail and enjoyed a peaceful, solo start to my day. But as I strolled, I couldn't help but think about my little adventurer, and what a great place this would be to expose her to a type of art she had never seen before. Not to mention, it's outdoors, with plenty of space to run and no one to bother like there is in a typical museum.

So this time when I visited, I had Harper and Andrew in tow. When we reached the Richard Nixon structure, she stopped dead in her tracks, assessed his facial expression and asked, "Why does he look mad? Or sad?" Was this an ample opportunity to speak to her candidly? Give a lecture on power, corruption, and spectacular falls? I watched my husband wrestle with how to answer the question, but before either of us could say anything, she said "Whatever" and skipped along to the huge elephant structure. We'll save the history lesson for our next visit.

The Vault at Freckle Salvage

Winthrop, Maine

Each month, Freckle Salvage, a gift shop off Route 202 in Winthrop, hosts a two-day, themed vintage market showcasing more than twenty different vendors and their curated finds. Past and upcoming themes at "The Vault" at Freckle Salvage include: endless summer, vintage menagerie, and perfect pairings. On the spring day I visited, the theme was garden party. With all vendors abiding by the theme, it truly looked like a greenhouse or flower farm had exploded within the six-thousand-square-foot former textile factory. Ornate vases with silk flowers, carefully constructed birdhouses with needle felted chickadees peeking out, and antique garden tools filled every nook. Even vintage finds that didn't necessarily fit the theme—like the vintage galvanized metal dairy box we took home—were filled with florals that blended with the garden party.

Freckle Salvage reveals their monthly themes (and sneak-peeks of the finds) on their Facebook page. If the timing is right, pop in to refresh your decor on your way upta camp.

Saco Heath Preserve

Saco, Maine

Harper calls the Saco Heath Preserve the "Wizard of Oz" trail. While you don't need a tornado to land here, the stark contrast of the peaceful trail compared to the busy main street where you'll find the trailhead does make it feel like you have been suddenly transported. A candy-colored, one-mile boardwalk winds through a raised coalesced bog, while butterflies and birds flutter throughout. It does feel remarkably similar to a certain yellow brick road. And if it wasn't for the quiet and serenity that shrouds the bog, it seems plausible a singing scarecrow might appear at any moment.

On our visit, when we turned a corner near the middle of the trail, we noticed an older couple lying flat on their stomachs. The couple was getting up close and personal with something along the edge of the wooden planks. As we approached, they waved for our daughter to come see. "It's a pitcher plant!" they said. "It's not every day you see a carnivorous plant!" Before Harper could ask what that long word was, she raced over to get a glimpse. Pitcher plants have deep, pitcher-shaped pouches containing fluid that attracts insects, and, once the insects are captured, the plant absorbs nutrients from their bodies. We all

Saco Health Preserve in Saco, Maine.

huddled around, staring at the lone pitcher plant waving in the wind, nestled among over one-thousand acres of heath.

Eventually, Harper decided that she didn't care and took off down the boardwalk singing "We're Off to See the Wizard."

Lubec Brewing Company

Lubec, Maine

On my first visit to Lubec Brewing Company, a microbrewery in the easternmost town in the United States, the topic du jour was what to make for a neighbor's birthday party. On one hand, a Lubec local had procured some extremely fresh fish from a fisherman down the street, while on the other hand, he's really known for his backyard BBQs. Making a decision on the main dish for his beloved pal's seventy-fifth birthday party was proving quite the headache so he decided to crowdsource among the beer lovers at the brewery. Ultimately, I encouraged him to keep it simple and stick with the burgers so he could really focus on enjoying the party and celebrate his friend. He agreed.

We were treated to a bright, warm spring day and found a perfect nook in their beer garden to take in views of Campobello Island just off in the distance beyond the Canadian border. For the hour we were there, dozens of locals swung by to fill their growlers, and every single person was greeted by first name. I overheard one patron share a story about the brewery's past Vinalhaven Lounge Meetings—essentially a listening club for those who love music recorded on vinyl.

It felt like time slowed down in that beer garden. It was as if within the walls of the brewery what actually mattered rose to the surface—friendship, humor, vinyl jams, and backyard celebrations. Though I wouldn't say it out loud at the risk of hitting my peak corniness, I did look around and think more than once: this is what they mean when they say "The way life should be."

Boothead Preserve

Lubec, Maine

The Bold Coast, a coastal stretch extending from Milbridge to the Canadian border community of Calais, is dotted with iconic wild blueberry barrens in every direction. The barrens are a deep, luscious blue in the summer, with the fields turning a flaming red in the fall when past peak. The barrens accompany you, as you wind your way to some of Maine's most majestic hiking trails scattered along the rugged coast, featuring dense forests, coastal bogs, moss-covered everything, and dramatic, steep panoramic ocean views. Out of all of the trail options—and trust me when I say the options are seemingly endless on the Bold Coast—Boothead Preserve, owned by the Maine Coast Heritage Trust, is one you should not miss.

The two-mile loop trail, on the easy side of moderate, is one Harper had no trouble completing. Within the seven-hundred acres of Boothead Preserve, you'll encounter plenty of attention stealers—upland forests, a raised peatland, cobblestone beaches, bright green moss, spongy green lichen, and coastal wetlands. But the heartbeat-skipping part comes once the trail eventually loops against the coast and tucks alongside a small cove with crashing turquoise blue waves to reveal a sublime slice of

Boothead Preserve in Lubec, Maine.

unspoiled, naturally stunning Downeast Maine. The view of Boot Cove occasionally sweeps through my thoughts—a place that permanently makes itself known in my memory bank. Once you see it, you'll never be without it.

Jasper Beach

Machiasport, Maine

Jasper Beach, tucked within Harbor Cove in Machiasport, is made up entirely of ocean-smoothed rocks of varying size and color, from pink marble-sized stones to light green fist-sized ones, and everything in between. There are so many stones on this beach that it's tough to wrap your brain around, each one a slightly different color, design, and shape. They are so smooth and perfectly round that they resemble rocks you'd find in a museum gift shop—the polished, lustrous ones next to the sparkly exposed crystals by the register.

As you traverse the beach, your feet will submerge, sinking beneath the rocks with each step while a sea song hums with each pull of a wave against the polished stones. And if you visit the beach during low tide, you'll be treated to gigantic arches formed out of the exposed bedrock along the perimeter, creating sea caves perfect for a game of hide and seek. The Bold Coast is already a lightly populated area—in Machiasport, the population hovers around a thousand—so the odds of you being solo on the beach are high. Time it right with the tide, comb for some of the smoothest sea glass you will ever find in Maine, and blissfully let the hours slip by.

ME Water Buffalo Company

Appleton, Maine

You know the expression, if you love something, set it free and if it comes back to you it was meant to be? That's sort of what happened with Jessica and Brian Farrar, owners of a water buffalo farm in the small town of Appleton, not far from Camden and about fifteen miles inland.

After years of raising water buffalo, a herd of twenty-seven to be exact, the Farrar Family sold all of their buffalo plus their farm to step away from the consuming, all-encompassing work of running a niche farm. Only eight short months later, however, they purchased new water buffalo and began again. Turns out, the old saying is true—when you love something that much, it's going to find a way to come back to you.

When I hopped out of my car for my scheduled thirty-minute farm tour, I was greeted by the family dog who gave me a proper sniffing before guiding me over to his owners. I found Jessica and Brian knee-deep in work building a new pig pen for the piglets arriving that week. They happily welcomed me and guided me up to the spacious barn to begin the tour. On the way, as we passed their other animals and made quick stops to say hello, one sweet baby goat cried out for Jessica as she drew near. Jessica had been bottle-feeding this little one for the past couple weeks and he was instantly soothed as soon as Jessica was close. As the dog faithfully circled her, the bunnies curled against her, the barn cat purred, and the goats cried as she passed—it was clear Jessica welcomed the role of mom for all of her beloved animals.

As soon as we entered the barn housing the water buffalo, they cocked their heads and turned to greet us. I'm not sure what I was expecting, but I was immediately taken aback by their size. As I moved toward these majestic beasts, with Jessica's permission, I gave one of the big girls some solid head scratches. Even more surprising than their size, was how affectionate they were—even Sassy, the buffalo that often gave Jessica attitude. Each buffalo would lean into me, savoring each caress, making the rest of the herd green with envy. They would crane their necks toward us and turn into lovey mush as soon as they felt our touch. I toured the small, inventive milking facility that the Farrars created (a lowered version built into the ground so that the buffalo were raised above them—no back pains for these milkers!) and enjoyed a front-row seat learning about their dairy products.

With its high butterfat content, water buffalo milk is used to create decadent, creamy cheeses, like burrata and fromage blanc, along with Sicilian-style gelato and cream-top yogurt. On warm summer nights, the Farrars host pizza nights featuring their homemade mozzarella di bufala. The farm has begun hosting summer camps for the youngest of farmers to get their hands dirty along with "farm stay glamping" for those looking to make a weekend out of their visit.

I understand that this farm raises buffalo for dairy and meat and there are inevitable trips to the slaughterhouse, but what I also know, and feel very confident about, is that the Farrars give these animals a full, happy life until then. And, from what I witnessed and what the past has shown, I think the Farrars would say the animals give back that exactly in return.

Meet Sarah Madeira Day

Cumberland Foreside, Maine
@sarahmadeiraday, @thismainehouse

When it comes to art, especially when you don't know a tremendous amount about it, everyone's advice is: "Just buy what you like!" Good advice in theory, go with what speaks to you. But what if nothing speaks to you? Or, what if what softly whispers your name is so outrageously beyond your budget that the whole art thing just stresses you out and you avoid making a choice? For, forever?

Andrew and I own a small house—but it features one large wall in our living room that has always befuddled me. It is large enough that I knew any piece of artwork that would properly fill the space would need to be pretty huge, which meant, of course, it would come with a hefty price tag. The wall is the focal point of the room and, although I am the farthest thing from an interior decorator, it was obvious that something, anything, needed to hang on that wall. I'd scour vintage stores, go cross-eyed looking at artwork online, and accept unsolicited advice from guests. Once in a while, I'd come across something online that drew me in, but I'd get to the checkout point, tally up the total of the print plus the framing costs, and slam my computer shut.

I had a friend over for dinner one night and as we stood staring at the wall together, she grabbed her phone, scrolled for a second, and handed it to me. She showed me a painting of Willard Beach—my beach, my daughter's stomping grounds, the beach that convinced Andrew and I to move to Maine after just a single week's vacation. Hues of soft pink, yellow, blue and green filled the screen. An available print fit the dimensions I needed and the colors complimented the rest of the room. It felt like it was specifically made for my wall. Still, I knew what came next—the moment of truth at checkout.

Turns out, no problem. What I have now learned about Sarah Madeira Day is that she is committed to making her art accessible for all. Her originals are for sale, but she also provides affordable reproduction unstretched prints. You can invest and secure a cherished, framed masterpiece for your home or you can buy a single print, grab a frame at Target, and gift it to a friend to commemorate a memory you shared together. And everything in between.

Sarah paints Maine. She paints places where she goes on adventures, places her kids play. Places like Sand Beach, Bradbury Mountain, Cranberry Island, and Somes Sound. Places that if you have visited, you likely have a tucked away, revered memory.

In addition to the perfect piece that now proudly hangs in my living room, other prints of her work are scattered throughout my house. I'm reminded of family adventures, inside jokes, and gratitude each time I walk by. I guess this is what they mean when they say art should speak to you.

....

Maine in Sarah's Words

A Favorite Maine Adventure

"Any trail off of the Long Pond pumping station in Southwest Harbor. Mile Rock, West Ridge Trail, Perpendicular Trail, all good. Taking a hike and then taking a swim is the best."

Last Meal on Earth Somewhere in Maine

"Thoroughfare in Yarmouth for two Gluten Free Impossible Burgers. The fries are not gluten free so I get two burgers for good measure."

A Person in Maine You Admire

"I think it is more Mainers as a collective that I admire. They are a savvy, creative, hardworking group of people that often seem to daylight as one thing and moonlight as another, juggling multiple jobs, full time or seasonal, to make living here work. It is the fortitude and honesty (good and bad) that you find in Mainers that is inspiring and unique to me. It's the state that lures you here and the people who keep you."

Why You Call Maine Home

"It's where I was born and it is the place that holds my heart."

....

Thoroughfare

Yarmouth, Maine

The perfect smash burgers at Thoroughfare on Main Street in Yarmouth were a result of the pandemic. Christian Hayes, owner of the Garrison, a revered fine-dining establishment less than a mile down the road, pivoted to takeout to keep that restaurant afloat. What came from these takeout days within the walls of The Garrison, was the concept (and menu) of Thoroughfare. Those early pandemic days feel like just yesterday and also a lifetime ago—a time when the highlight of the week, at least in our household, was getting takeout somewhere on Friday night. We tried new places, supported old favorites, and ordered way ahead of time. The days that felt the darkest were made brighter by some of those who were hit the hardest—people in the restaurant industry.

Thoroughfare is technically fast food—you order at the window and they quickly turn around your meal. But it's elevated fast food, food you don't feel bad about after you eat it. The food is clearly prepared with care, skill, and quality, well-sourced ingredients—but somehow it still evokes memories of childhood fast-food runs. However, I don't ever remember seeing something like Thoroughfare's Kimmy Gibbs sandwich (fried haddock, sweet soy glaze, kimchi, pickled onion, kewpie mayo, iceberg) on the fast-food menus from when I was a kid—those were usually just some semblance of an unidentifiable white fish slapped between stale buns.

Enjoying sunshine on their outside patio, we finished our smash burgers (complete with two patties, American cheese, pickles, iceberg lettuce, minced onions, and their special sauce) while Harper polished off her vanilla malt milkshake—refusing to share even a sip.

Tumbledown Mountain

Weld, Maine

People You Will Meet At Tumbledown Mountain:

A grizzled eighty-year-old mountain hiker tackling Tumbledown for his tenth (or so) time. It's different now, without his grandkids in tow. It'll take him longer to reach the summit, but it'll definitely be quieter along the way. He'll likely, as in our case, stop in his tracks as you pass, get down to your five-year-old's eye level and say "I admire you." It'll help boost your little one's confidence right when she needs a pep talk before some challenging rock scrambling.

College kids from Bates who breeze through the trail even if they stayed out all night. They'll pass you, gossiping about what went down last night, as you try to play it cool and pretend you aren't panting as they glide by.

The mom who decided everyone was going outside today. She is dripping in sweat, beet red, and wishing she packed water (or anything for that matter). She sits on a rock listening to her teenagers complain, wondering what's really so wrong with screen time, anyway.

The solo hiker tackling Tumbledown for the first time; backpack filled with all essentials (and then some), a good camera and an even-better attitude. They'll float by, rejuvenated by the silence that comes with hiking alone, completely intoxicated by their surroundings.

The older couple, enjoying a beautiful Sunday morning together, who will lie to you. "Are we about halfway?" you'll ask. They'll eye your wide-eyed little one, look at her determined, tired parents, and say, "Yes, about halfway."

Harper on Tumbledown Mountain in Weld, Maine.

You are not nearly half way.

And the young couple with a toddler to whom you will subsequently lie to on your way down. "Yes, about halfway."

People like these, and others, will be with you at the top of the mountain where everyone will find an alpine pond (or mountain tarn) nestled between Tumbledown and Little Jackson Mountain. Just when your legs begin to feel a little rubbery from the climb, it will appear and you'll forget how hard it was to get there. You can reach it from the four-mile out-and-back trail we pursued—the Brook Trail—or one of the more rigorous loop hikes in the ten-plus miles of connecting trails. There is no picture I have seen of the pond that does it justice.

You won't be the only person at Tumbledown Mountain. But if you were, you wouldn't get to give a countdown to the off-duty cops and their K9 before they jumped into the cold pond. Or smile at the two twenty-somethings on their first date dipping their feet in the water. Or watch proud kids enjoy smushed peanut butter and jellies at the peak. These people, from all walks of life and hiking experience scattered throughout the trails, gives this three-thousand-foot mountain an undeniable heartbeat.

IN RAINCOATS

Princess Picnic at Riverside Lavender Farm

Steep Falls, Maine

I remembered half way down our street that I didn't have my phone. I turned around, ran back to the house, and grabbed it while Harper waited patiently in the car. I found it on the charger in my bedroom, and realized I hadn't checked it since waking up a few hours ago. With my phone secured and *Encanto* now filling the car, I caught an animated rendition of "The Family Madrigal" in the rearview mirror.

I had spent the morning completing a one-thousand-piece puzzle with Harper. We finally finished around nine, after multiple days working on it, and threw a little dance party in the living room to celebrate. We had some Scratch Bakery muffins for breakfast and talked about what first grade might be like next year. With Andrew away for the weekend, I reminded her that I had planned a surprise just for her and it was time to get dressed for our adventure. Normally, getting dressed is met with a few whines, but not this time—she booked it to her room in record time.

For most of her life, I admittedly have been miles away at times. Not literally—I can count on one hand the number of times in a year that I have been away from her physically. But on most days, I have been mentally somewhere else. I never took maternity leave when she was born and, although I absolutely did not need to, I conducted a client consultation call from my hospital bed the day after she was born. Owning a small business means there is always something you can be doing—you don't always have to, but if you don't, what if you did? What if you put in that extra couple hours—would it move the needle?

Work never turned off for me because I cared too deeply about it. Every component that filled me with pride—from my incredible students to my talented employees to the business itself—required time, attention, and love. All of my lines were constantly blurred; my life was my work. I counted myself one of the lucky ones to love what I did for a living, but at what cost? There certainly wasn't a day when I didn't check my email the second I woke up, much less forget about my phone for an entire morning.

As the chorus picked up for "We Don't Talk About Bruno" with Harper belting her little heart out, it hit me—maybe *this* is my redo. I'm listening to her more intently, doing my best to say "yes" as much as I can, getting to savor a year when she is still young enough to think I am cool. This year can be, and will be, about her, too.

When we arrived at Riverside Lavender Farm, a full thirteen acres with over seven thousand lavender plants just west of Sebago Lake, we were promptly greeted by Tammy Braun, one of the farm's owners. Carrying a tray loaded with homemade

The Princess Picnic at Riverside Lavender Farm in Steep Falls, Maine.

lavender lemonade and cookies, she guided us along with a few other families down the hill to our Princess Picnic. I hadn't told Harper much about this adventure, but when she saw a basket full of tutus, it didn't matter what we were doing.

At the Princess Picnic at Riverside Lavender Farm, kiddos are treated to a thirty-minute picnic next to the farm's seemingly endless purple rows of lavender and are allowed to borrow (or purchase at the end) a handmade tutu or cape to wear during the petite garden party. A complimentary homemade lavender crown is given to each visitor. My daughter had four glasses of lemonade (I was leaning into saying yes and being the greatest mom ever—okay?) and two homemade lavender cookies. Now on a sugar high, we made our way toward Tammy's herd of Nigerian dwarf goats for some playtime.

The kids and the goats amused each other while Tammy entertained the adults by sharing stories about the farm, their private beach along the Saco River, the onsite camping opportunities, and her and her husband's plans for their upcoming retirement. She encouraged us to come back in a few weeks for a glimpse and sniff of the fragrant lavender during peak season, when it becomes what she described as a "photographer's dream."

After prying Harper away from the goats, we said goodbye to Tammy and climbed back in the car.

"Fun morning?" I asked.

"Best morning," she said. "Best mom."

It was clearly the lemonade, cookies, and tutus that secured this sweet sentiment, but I chose to believe it.

Meet Claire Guyer & Richard Lee

Portland, Maine
@littlebrotherchinesefood

If you are tempted to visit Maine because of the embarrassment of riches that is our food scene, groovy. I'm sure you've done your research, read the lists, prioritized your favorite destinations. You should make a plan and try to eat at as many restaurants as you can possibly fit into your itinerary—even if that means doubling up on meals. But I'll let you in on a little secret, something you won't find mentioned in a "Best Restaurants in Portland, Maine" roundup or the *New York Times* must-visit restaurant list—some of the best dumplings made from scratch are in Portland, but you can't make a reservation to enjoy them.

If you're local, and like my family, Little Brother Chinese Food dumplings make it into your weekly lineup of meals. You can find them at various markets throughout Maine or in my personal freezer, which is always stocked with them. Two of their jiaozi, the pork and napa cabbage (a recipe passed down from Richard's grandmother and aunt) and the beef and broccoli, have caused rifts in our family when someone steals the last one at dinnertime. And no one is allowed to touch my La Jiao Jiang Hot Sauce from Little Brother that I, quite literally, put on everything—the crunchy fried garlic and red onion hot sauce drapes over my eggs, bagels, rice, ice cream (not kidding), and, of course, dumplings.

Little Brother Chinese Food operates out of Fork Food Lab in South Portland, a nonprofit food business incubator and shared commercial kitchen that has a mission to continue to grow Maine's local food economy. I've gone to events in this space and participated in cooking classes, and the energy that radiates from the floorboards to the ceiling is soulful, creative, and filled with collective ambition.

In addition to the dumplings churned out from Fork Food Lab, Richard is also an artist, Claire a sewist—among, I'm sure, other creative ventures. Their artistic endeavors don't just fill their dumplings; rather, their artistry is scattered throughout Maine in the forms of mixed-media paintings or handmade quilt coats. Their bios, and perhaps business cards (do people still have those?) have a plus sign. They are dumpling makers + creatives, plus business owners, plus valued community members, plus bakers, plus husband and wife, plus lovers of hospitality.

I'm working on allowing myself to have plus signs. Giving myself the space to not only rediscover, but intersect, the many parts of me. And I'll do this while I gorge on pork and cabbage dumplings + La Jiao Jiang Hot Sauce + Little Dumpling Chicken Fried Rice + pumpkin and spiced tofu jiaozi + anything else Claire and Richard come up with.

Maine in Claire & Richard's Words

A Favorite Maine Adventure

"While I [Claire] was in college, I spent my summers working on Monhegan Island. I still have so much fondness for the island—I made a lot of friends who still make it their year-round home—and for the place itself. Like most seasonal workers there, I was mostly busy working, but on my rare days off, I would walk the trail that goes around the island. It's one of the most beautiful places in the world. There's a gorgeous pine forest, a lighthouse, beaches, and dramatic cliffs that look out on nothing but the Atlantic Ocean for miles and miles and miles. There's not another place like it, and I count myself lucky to have been able to contribute to it."

Last Meal on Earth Somewhere in Maine

"This is so tough. There's a few things that come to mind—mostly things that we would insist out of town visitors try before we let them get on a plane."

Claire's childhood go-to that still hits the spot every time: Popcorn shrimp dinner at Moody's Diner in Waldoboro

The absolutely decadent cheese and jam biscuits from Tandem Coffee in Portland.

A slice of pizza from the bakery at Miccuci's Market in Portland.

A sauerkraut hot dog from Wasses Hot Dogs in Rockland.

The complete perfection of a fresh bagel from Scratch Bakery in South Portland (best enjoyed on Willard Beach right around the corner).

Any sandwich from Rose Foods or Ramona's in Portland, accompanied by half-sour pickles from Morse's Sauerkraut in Waldoboro.

A Person in Maine You Admire

"We're part of Fork Food Lab, Maine's only food-business incubator. Food trucks, caterers, direct-to-consumer food manufacturers, and a diverse array of people of all ages and experiences share kitchen space under the watchful eye of Corrinne Thompkins, our general manager. I think that Fork, and Corinne specifically, are probably doing more to develop the food scene in this state than anyone else. Between connecting local suppliers with members, creating collective buying programs, fundraising, organizing events, endlessly advocating for all of Fork's members, and managing a huge space used by more than fifty businesses with endlessly diverse needs, she's really the glue that holds the whole place together."

Why You Call Maine Home

"I [Claire] grew up here, and despite living elsewhere for a long time, I felt called to come back. There's nowhere else with the abundance of natural beauty that you find here. I've also been a fan of swimming in the ocean since I was little—my body just seems to crave the cold, super-salty water. Bringing Richard here was so fun because I get to fall in love with it all again through his eyes. We met while we were both living in Chicago—where he lived his whole life before moving here. I've been introducing him to all my favorite little beaches, taking him sailing with my dad in Rockland, going for walks at all the best spots in and around Portland, but I think the farmer's market really has his cook's heart one-hundred-percent charmed. I think the profusion of Southeast Asian food in southern Maine was also an early selling point. He maybe wishes there was a little more Northern-Style Chinese food like he grew up with, but we're working on changing that."

••

Monhegan Island

Monhegan, Maine

Every inch of Monhegan is begging to be photographed or painted. This island, ten miles off the coast, has beckoned and transfixed artists for more than one hundred and fifty years. Monhegan, with a year-round population of about sixty people, is a quaint fishing village, its docks dotted with fishermen and their traps. Its enormous granite cliffs and roughly three hundred fifty acres of conserved land provide endless artistic stimulation.

As soon as I unloaded from the hour-long boat ride from Port Clyde on a late-spring morning, I could feel it. Creative energy filled my veins and a wash of inspiration poured over me. A story began to develop with each corner I turned, and I couldn't help but see the island through the lens of my own preferred art form—a play. Vignettes of year-round islanders blending with tourists, of tired bodies resting along the cliff-lined trails, and of winding dirt roads provided the perfect scenes for my three-act, intermission-free, nonlinear, sans-traditional-narrative-arc play I spun throughout the day. I don't think I would sell many tickets to this production, but a good time was had by this pretend playwright.

Monhegan Island.

Scene 1: Banana, but with an M

I hang a right off of the boat landing to make my way to The Fish House. Fish tacos secured, I'm lucky to nab a coveted picnic table at the beach overlooking adjacent Manana

Island. Pronounced like banana with an M, this island is just three quarters of a mile in length and only half a mile wide. In between bites of pan-fried haddock tacos, I notice goats grazing on the uninhabited island. These goats, which spend winters in Kennebunk, are rowed to the island in the spring to enjoy their summer months roaming Manana. The goats remind me of the story I heard about Ray Phillips, the hermit of Manana Island, who spent more than forty years here in a home made of driftwood on the cliff facing Monhegan. He had no human companions, but he had a faithful herd of sheep and a large goose named Donald Duck to keep him company. In my mind, the entire first act would consist of Ray abruptly fleeing the hustle of New York City, committing to a life of simplicity, and combatting any loneliness with occasional mainland trips to have a night on the town.

Scene 2: To the Shipwreck

There are roughly twelve miles of zig-zagging trails on Monhegan. I knew I wanted to see the *D.T. Sheridan* shipwreck at Lobster Cove, so I chose the Whitehead Trail, which weaves through thick forests before eventually meeting the rugged Cliff Trail—with a view of Gull Cove and Gull Rock—and finally landing at the Lobster Cove Trail. On the way to the trailhead, I passed the school house (a one-room school with fewer than ten students enrolled from preschool to eighth grade), the Monhegan Lighthouse (built in 1824), and struck up conversations with the painters along the edges of the dusty dirt road who were reveling in a gorgeous day. Along the Whitehead Trail, birders with binoculars were scattered, beaming as they spotted birds I would have never known were there. Upon reaching Whitehead Cliff, it became obvious why so many were paused here to rest—tired legs, for one thing—but the wind gets knocked out of you upon that first glimpse of the crystal clear crashing surf and dramatic drops. I joined the entangled couples, photographers, and intrepid families to catch my breath and ogle the views. This part of the play has no dialogue, just a dramatic underscore while the waves do their thing.

Nearing the edge of the southeastern shore of Lobster Cove, I spy the first remnants of the shipwreck. In November 1948, a thick fog circled the island, causing the coal-carrying tug to wreck. Over the years, pieces have rusted to perfection and are scattered throughout the cove, with a large hunk of the hull at the center. A flashback scene in the play provides us with a glimpse into the day of her wreck to watch the quick-thinking captain, Raymond Pix, bring all members of the crew safely to the shore.

Scene 3: Pale Ale and Pistachio

The only thing that would make this hike better, as is the case with most hikes in my experience, is a cold beer at the end—a reward in the form of a cool, crisp IPA or Pale Ale. As luck would have it, and likely with some thoughtful, deliberate placement on their part, Monhegan Brewing is just steps away from the end of the trail. Before you see the sign for the brewery, you'll hear laughter and chatter pulling you in the right direction. When you arrive, you'll be greeted by sunkissed faces filling their outside beer garden while busy employees mill throughout, delivering gifts in the form of beers.

Surveying the scene while savoring their aptly named Lobster Cove Pale Ale, I find a charming landscape of people. I notice an older woman, perched at a high-top table close to the entrance, turning the pages of a novel. I imagine her to be a local who arrives right at opening to snag her favorite shady spot. She's seated close to a jovial gentleman who is sharing memories of Monhegan with what seem to be some visiting friends. There are photographers going through their images of the day while sampling a tasting flight. A newborn baby crying, perhaps on a first getaway that won't be remembered, except by two nervous, tired parents. Mary and Matt, two of the three owners, are making conversation, delivering beers, and running the ship. And me, ordering my second pale ale before walking back to the boat. I think this would have to be a musical number in my otherwise straight play—it just seems ripe with opportunity for an uptempo, comedic song to erupt in the bustling garden with beers overflowing from mugs.

Winding back through the village, I spy a sign for ice cream at The Novelty. I should keep going, I think, to make my boat—but I see Pistachio on the menu and throw caution to the wind. With a double cone and sticky hands, I rush to the boat and manage to secure a spot on the top deck. The goats are still roaming on Manana, familiar faces fill the boat for the return home, and I snap one final picture.

And: scene. Blackout.

Oyster River Winegrowers

Warren, Maine

If only I owned a flapper dress. I'll be on the hunt for one now since I know exactly where it will make its debut. I'll be the only one dressed in 1920s fashion, perhaps, but I don't think anyone would bat an eye at this all-natural winery near Rockland when I saunter in.

Andrew and I walked into the barn on a misty Saturday afternoon as Ella Fitzergald played softly over the speakers. I don't know if these cherished, jazzy tunes are always spinning, but I'd like to think so. And perhaps it was just in my imagination, but I swear the bar patrons turned to greet us with a nod, softly tipping their caps in our direction before returning attention back to their wine. We moseyed up to the bar, with a barn cat circling in and out of our legs, and grabbed a glass of their Morphos—a natural wine made from merlot that is allowed to ferment in the bottle to create a fizzy rosé. It was a tough choice between the five others available for tasting that day, but when it was time for a refill, I couldn't part with the delicate, refreshing pink wine.

Mismatched chairs, vintage couches, and rocking chairs are spread throughout the barn; there are a couple of books here and a couple of old board games there. Bessie Smith is singing now, Andrew and I tuck into the corner to share a pink loveseat and my mind immediately wanders to our days of dating in NYC. There, to experience something like this, we'd have to knock three times in a fake telephone booth, say some semblance of a code word to then be let into an underground, overcrowded speakeasy with loud jazz standards playing and overpriced drinks pouring. The ambience Oyster River Winegrowers creates is something people try so hard to replicate, but it can only exist in an old barn, in Maine, in a winery that for the first seven seasons, had their vineyards cultivated only by draft horse power and by hand.

Oyster River Winegrowers in Warren, Maine.

Their wine is available in their Camden store year-round and their tasting room in the romantic Warren barn is open on a limited schedule in the summer. In between my visits, I'll be perfecting my jitterbug.

Reid State Park

Georgetown, Maine

If you haven't been to Reid State Park on a windy day, I can tell you, definitively, that you are missing out. And if you haven't been to Reid State Park *ever*, consider this your invite.

The seven-hundred-and-seventy-acre park near Bath is best known for its wide sandy beach (two beaches, actually; Half Mile and Mile Beach) and their respective sand dunes—which are both something of a rarity in Maine. Bookending Mile Beach are Griffith Head and Todd's Point, rocky prominent points overlooking the park and offering views of Seguin Island, The Cuckolds, Hendricks Head, and sweeping views of the Atlantic Ocean. Family-friendly walking trails fill the park, and you will be hard pressed to find a spot that doesn't take your breath away.

When the weather forecast predicts heavy wind, no matter the season, I book it to Reid State Park. Partly because the waves will become something straight out of a movie, but mostly to catch a glimpse of some fearless, impressive people. Surfers flock to one of the top-ranked surfing beaches in New England regardless of what the thermometer reads. I like to sit perched on a rock and mentally rate the surfer's performance, as if I have any idea what I am talking about or have any credentials to do so.

Momo's Cheesecake Bakery

Ellsworth, Maine

I worry that people don't believe me when I tell them about Momo's because it's like a magical mirage, a too-good-to-be-true situation. A cheesecake shop open twenty-four hours that operates on the honor system? Yeah, right.

But oh, it's true. When you pull up to Momo's house (that's right, the store is located on her property in Ellsworth), your eyes will be drawn to the bright red garage. Once inside, no matter how cool, calm, and collected you might think you are, you will turn into a giddy, bubbly kid. You'll become utterly indecisive when scanning the fridges filled with cheesecake flavors like Lemon Blueberry, Cherry Garcia, Pumpkin, Oreo, and Turtle. You may end up with four slices of cheesecake for yourself and your husband may laugh when you get back in the car. You may be on your way to a hike and have no need for four slices of cheesecake, but who's to say?

So, if a craving for decadent cheesecake calls to you in the middle of the night, first thing in the morning, or right before heading to Acadia National Park for an arduous hike, you are in luck. Bring cash, sign the guestbook, and know you won't be the only one enjoying their cheesecake the second you hop back into the car.

Spurwink River to Higgins Beach

Scarborough, Maine

For the past week, I suffered more than a few sleepless nights. Those nights I ended up on the couch to avoid waking Andrew and lay staring at the ceiling or watching the clock, listening to my dog snore beside me.

The most maddening part is that for the first time ever, I am essentially stripped of all of the day-to-day stressors and triggers. No more Sunday scaries, no more late-night teaching, no more useless worries sending me into a tailspin, no more clogged inboxes. I should be hitting the pillow and easily drifting off into a splendid slumber.

With summer in Maine now at our fingertips, our social calendar is seeing a serious boost. Our guest room is filled most weekends and laid-back barbeques fill most weeknights. On these summer evenings, I find myself fluttering around, making small talk, checking drinks, and not staying in a single conversation too long. I know what I am avoiding, and I know my husband does, too.

It's not anyone's fault, they're just curious. The obligatory "How's work?" question naturally follows directly after the "How are you?" question. These questions keep me up. Even for the people I know well, who know I left my contract in January, suddenly stutter or reframe the question once they realize they are talking to me.

It's in these uncomfortable moments that I've realized how much I depended on the label that I, and others, created for myself. This label was stuck on when I was just six years old and played my first part at a performing-arts camp. It was sewn on more firmly when I began teaching acting in college and was officially branded when I started my audition-coaching business. I'm a performing artist. That's what people expect from me, and frankly, want me to be. It's easiest, sometimes, to understand and process who a person is by what they do. When people ask "What do you do?" what they are really trying to figure out is either a way to relate to you or judge you.

I used my label to my advantage most of my life and, much like the profession I found myself in, I played the part depending on the audience. When I would have dinner with the partners at my husband's law firm, wondering if I was wearing and saying the right thing, I was a business owner. When I was desperately trying to "make it" in New York City, pursuing any and every audition, often against my better judgment, I was unshakably an actress. When hosting a college webinar for hundreds of students, I was the best acting teacher you'd ever have. To me, my worth was in my labels, and to every audience, I wanted to be worthy.

And now late at night, when my mind begins its nightly race, I'm realizing that without these labels, I don't really know who I am. Without my badges of honor to point to, I don't have much to say. I suffer this feeling that what is underneath—the me without any medals—isn't of any value.

On this day, I drank an extra cup of coffee and pretended to feel fine as Andrew and I loaded our canoe on top of the car. It was a long weekend, Harper was occupied for the day and I was determined to take advantage of the bonus day with Andrew. There was not a cloud in the sky when we got to the put-in off Route 77 in Scarborough. We unloaded with ease and set off for a new-to-us paddle.

The Spurwink River winds through marshes, offering glimpses of great blue herons, snowy egrets, and terns diving into the water and emerging with their mouths full of their finds. The trip through the marshes is about two miles, and then you start to see a change in the water as you approach the open ocean. You'll see Higgins Beach on your right, likely crawling with happy beachgoers, and, just as the river gets swallowed into the sea, there is a little sandy stretch of the beach to the right where you can park your canoe or kayak for a bit.

We hopped out of the canoe and walked along the shore at low tide. The trip down was a breeze, literally—the wind gently pushed us for the entirety, along with the tide, and the whole two miles only took us about twenty-five minutes with little paddling needed. On Higgins Beach, we stumbled upon the remains of a schooner named *Middleton* from an 1897 shipwreck. A chunk of her hull, covered in seaweed and sea moss, lies poking out from below the wet sand more than one hundred years later. When the tide is high, you would never know it was there.

We clasped hands and strolled along the edge of the water, letting the waves cover our feet as we walked.

"Didn't sleep again?" Andrew asked. Clearly, I wasn't covering it up as well as I thought. I shook my head and we walked in silence.

When we loaded back into the canoe for our return trip, the wind was absolutely no longer on our side. Nor was the tide. We braced ourselves, pushed out into the water and immediately began a hard, deep paddle against the waves.

"You know, you're always a great mom, but the past couple months, you've been an incredible mom," Andrew said from the back of the canoe. "Thank you. She feels it."

With my arms beginning to burn, I focused on the water in front of me, tearing up a bit from either the exhaustion or from Andrew's uncanny ability to always know what's brewing inside my congested brain.

"And I really needed this today. So thank you for convincing me," he said. "Thank you for always convincing me."

He does need reminders to step away from work and, although I often feel guilty when I head out on my adventures this year, I'm committed to making sure his moments outside of his screen time are when he actually lives.

As we finally reached calmness on the water, finding some relief for our back and shoulders, he said, "You're going to figure it out. Keep going."

Back at home, I pulled up my adventure list on my phone and added our canoe journey—but I didn't stop after I added the date and a few quick observations. Much more poured out of me—the distinct smell of the river, the fearless blue heron that swam a bit too close to the canoe, the hot sand under our feet. I made note of my husband's relaxed, soft voice that was noticeably different when miles away from his laptop. The trickle of sweat that escaped from my forehead and ran down my cheek. In a fury, I also tackled my least favorite question, in the comfort of knowing no one would hear it: What do I do?

I'm on my own gap year—eat, pray, loving my way through Maine, exploring new places that were never on my radar. I'm finally meeting my neighbors, getting to know them below the surface, and talking with strangers, soaking in the stories they share. I've gotten back into cooking and we are eating a lot healthier in our house. To offset that, I've been baking every weekend with my daughter. I'm planning camps, after-school activities, playdates, and taking care of pick-ups and drop-offs.

I'm perfecting my French braid for pigtails. I'm making an effort to donate more intentionally, more frequently. I'm making sure my family goes outside everyday and gets out of our comfy nook of the world. I'm making a change because I woke up one day uninspired, unmotivated, and sad. I'm realizing, with certainty, people aren't only one thing when they grow up.

And I write. I'm writing. I think I'm writing a book.

Glidden Point Oyster Farm

Edgecomb, Maine

I want to like oysters so bad. So desperately bad. It's maddening to me that I don't enjoy them like I love raw fish, but despite my best efforts and continued torturous, self-imposed tastings, I just can't get into them. I have a visceral reaction when I sample them and despite countless suggestions on the best way to enjoy them, shared favorite recipes and never saying no when one is offered, I haven't been able to successfully trick myself into thinking I am an oyster lover.

But I just can't stop going to Glidden Point. This oyster farm, which has been growing Maine oysters in the Damariscotta River for more than thirty years, continues to beckon me, despite my aversion.

I've planned countless friend meetups here, taken my in-laws during one of their visits to Maine, and often go solo. Additionally, you can pay to take a walking tour where a member of the Glidden Point team will walk with you along the banks of the Damariscotta River, talk through their oyster growing techniques, and give you a shucking lesson. After the thirty-minute stroll, wine, beer, snacks, and, of course, oysters are waiting for you to enjoy on their expansive deck overlooking the river.

Glidden Point is the epitome of a perfect Maine summer afternoon. In an hour or two, you can gain some knowledge about the oyster industry, soak in some rays by the water, maybe try a new food truck and definitely enjoy some of the best oysters in the world. Or so I'm told.

Great Pond

Cape Elizabeth, Maine

Unless you are a Cape Elizabeth resident, and one of the thirty-two lucky people who secure a boat storage permit in a yearly lottery drawing, you'll have to walk two hundred yards with your canoe before reaching the put-in spot on Great Pond. Besides the occasional sweat bead that might trickle down your face, you won't find much else to complain about, though, as you make your way down the forested, pastoral path.

Andrew and I fill our canoe with snacks and stick Harper in the middle to munch. At Great Pond, the largest body of freshwater in Cape Elizabeth, we never actually end up doing a tremendous amount of paddling, it's a place we mostly drift and observe. There are hidden nooks, surrounded by tall reeds where you might spot a turtle or a beaver. Lily pads dot the way, birds sing from what seems like every branch above, and friendly fellow paddlers wave as they glide by. Plan to drift for an hour or two and play a series of "I Spy" games or grab your ice skates in winter to cruise along the frozen paradise.

Harper's favorite part of Great Pond comes after the canoeing. Once all of the snacks are devoured and our legs are in need of some stretching, we'll load out and get the canoe back to the car near the Fenway Road entrance. Once secure, our little lady will dart back to the trailhead to begin the out and back trail that bends around the eastern shores of the pond. We'll trail her on the bog bridges that cover wetlands, the intricate elevated boardwalks constructed over Alewife Brook and find her (momentarily) pausing to take in views from a high bluff that overlooks the sparkling pond near the end of the trail.

If you're thinking, wow, a canoe trip and a trail all in one afternoon with no tantrums—that's one determined and amazing kiddo. You'd be right, for the most part. But one tiny detail, one little morsel of motivation or a small bribe if you will, awaits at the end of the trail. Across Bowery Beach Road, where the trail will land you, is Kettle Cove Creamery and Shack (open Mother's Day to Labor Day) that happens to have delicious ice cream and beach food.

I know no better motivation to keep little legs moving than a drippy ice cream cone.

Meet Ryan & Devon Wheeler

Newry, Maine
@puzzlemountainbakery

Just before reaching Grafton Notch State Park, where some of Maine's finest hiking trails reside, you might notice a string of cars pulled off to the side of Bear River Road. It's not because of a moose sighting or a secret swimming hole—it's to grab homemade treats at a tiny roadside bakery that makes the ultimate summit reward. With arms full of fruit jams, coveted cookies and berry pies, you won't find a cashier to check you out, however, because Puzzle Mountain Bakery, a quintessential Maine business in operation since 1999, functions on the honor system. Relying on the good will and honesty of their customers, patrons are free to grab what they'd like and leave cash in the payment box (or, new in the past couple years, shoot over a quick Venmo).

I had never made it to Puzzle Mountain Bakery before this year, slowly developing a pretty extensive mental checklist of must-try recommendations. The maple cookies, unanimously, were at the top of everyone's list, with some friends warning of their power—once you try them, that's it, you have to find a way to have more. They sell traditional Maine staples with flavors you'd expect from Vacationland—whoopie pies, blueberry everything, maple infusions—but with their own, family-derived twists.

Before collecting my treasures, I popped down the hill to the onsite bakery to chat with Ryan Wheeler, one of the owners. We connected over email a few days earlier and, although he'd be baking and restocking the stand solo that day, he graciously welcomed me despite his before-the-sun wakeup to get the pies in the oven.

Ryan was working on a pie crust when I popped in. With flour flying in the air, Ryan didn't skip a single beat in our conversation while his hands methodically worked the dough. He was buoyant and confident, efficiently churning out pies while sharing stories of the bakery's inception. In between delicate folds of the buttery crust, I learned about his mother, Mary Jo Kelly, who after becoming captivated by the idea of selling baked goods on the honor system, started what would become Puzzle Mountain Bakery with just a few pies for sale under a single umbrella along the side of the road.

Like Mary Jo Kelly, I'm smitten with the idea of an honor system bakery. The concept is, of course, so very Maine, requiring a mutual trust between consumer and baker. And, while the stand isn't completely theft proof, some of the worst offenders are the black bears that can't resist a freshly baked berry pie. On the day I visited, after counting cash for their tallied totals, I saw multiple families leave more than required—because on top of being thankful for an assortment of treats, it inherently feels good to be trusted. To know that if left to your own devices, you'll do the right thing. And this idea, which Mary Jo Kelly had right from the beginning, helps build and cultivate community in the place we love so much. A trust network built around flaky, golden brown pies. Maine, and its people, at their finest.

But an honor system bakery along the side of the road only works if the goodies are worth the drive. Luckily, you can taste the tradition, the inherited dream with over a decade's worth of love, still baked into Ryan and Devon's reimagined, expanded recipes—making them not just worth the journey, but instantly habit forming. I ate two of the maple cream cookies before ten and promptly hid the third one at home so I didn't have to share it.

The treats are divine, along with the business model. Ryan and Devon will continue to put trust in their neighbors, while I'll continue to trust that those maple cream cookies will always be there.

Maine in Ryan & Devon's Words

A Favorite Maine Adventure

"Our family's favorite trail is Step Falls in Grafton Notch because it is nearby and an easy hike for our son and dog with a view you can't beat. We are lucky to have this in our backyard. There is a rock on the water that we pass on our way up and Asher, our son, must stop every time, he calls it his yoga rock.

"Ryan and Asher's favorite adventure is hiking Ryan's great-grandfather's mica mine, the Wheeler Mine in West Bethel. They love digging for gemstones and enjoying the great outdoors overlooking the town of Bethel on top of the mountain or taking a kayak ride down the river.

Last Meal on Earth Somewhere in Maine

"Our last meal on Earth would be by far a lobster roll from Erica's in Harpswell. They have the best lobster—it's so sweet. Devon enjoys the lobster with just butter and Ryan likes his with mayo and lettuce—both on a slightly toasted bun—yum!"

A Person in Maine You Admire

"We admire Patrick Dempsey, we do not know him, but we believe he gives a lot back to the state of Maine through his contributions in the healthcare field. It's nice to see people who have successfully made it come home to their roots to try and help those less fortunate as much they can."

Why You Call Maine Home
"We call Maine our home because this is where we grew up and a lot of our family still lives here. Maine is a place we feel safe, a place to enjoy all four seasons and the beauty of nature."

Step Falls Preserve

Newry, Maine

There are adventures that get stored away for that perfect someday. Someday when I'll be in the area, someday when the weather is right, someday when I get it together to make it happen. I had visited Step Falls Preserve—a twenty-four-acre preserve in Western Maine near Grafton Notch State Park—solo in the past during an off-season chilly day and vowed to bring my family back when it was warm enough to fully enjoy it. You can't truly experience or appreciate Step Falls from the sidelines, you need to get right up in the middle of the action.

The someday arrived in the form of a sunny day in June, a birthday party cancellation, and a newly minted totally free day on our hands. With a sun-screened kiddo and panting pup in the backseat, we made the drive to Newry first thing in the morning.

The parking at Step Falls is fairly limited, which I appreciate. It was still early, however, so we were able to easily grab a spot and begin the just over a mile out-and-back trail along the gushing falls. Lined with spruce, balsam fir, and hemlock trees, the trail grows significantly steeper and a little more difficult

Step Falls Preserve in Newry, Maine.

toward the end. But the higher you climb, the bigger the payoff. From the top of the falls, which have an approximate 250-foot drop, you'll see a steep, descending series of cascades and pools. Because this is one of the highest falls in Maine, you'll also be treated to exquisite views of the mountains that surround you.

But the fun part really begins when you get to pick which section of the trail to divert away from to do some waterfall splashing. We tried out a few sections, finally settling on one that had a handful of small pools to wade in with one plunge pool deep enough to fully swim in. The granite rocks have eroded over time, creating smooth, natural water slides that we all—including the pooch—took a turn sliding down. Laughter from other families ricocheted off the granite and shrieks of joy from bodies gliding into cold pools echoed in the trees. Nowhere to be but here, at a free, natural waterpark, nestled in the trees with my favorite people all day. Bliss.

Summer Sunsets at Thompson's Point

Portland, Maine

While I have never actually made it to the sunset portion of this event (young kids and bedtimes, you know), that's only one of the reasons that make this gathering something to look forward to each week. When the weather starts to warm up and Mainers hesitantly, but hopefully, put their coats away, Thursdays and Fridays start to become a lot more fun with the help of Thompson's Point. A riverside venue that hosts summer concerts, festivals, winter ice skating and more—I find myself here quite often throughout the course of a year.

During Summer Sunsets, food trucks line the perimeter of the outdoor space, bands take the stage, dogs look for head scratches, and adult beverages flow from the outside bar. You'll run into friends, neighbors, frenemies—everyone—all from your coveted picnic blanket spot. You'll let your kid run free, you'll stuff as many Mr. Tuna hand rolls into your face as possible, and you'll feel pretty thankful to have another Maine summer on your hands.

Meet Lauren Gauthier

Portland, Maine

@littleeasysnoballs

First things first—a snoball is not a snowcone. A snowcone is made with crunchy, granular ice, often with just a few flavor varieties (like the blue raspberry flavor I liked during childhood even though it turned my mouth an aggressive bright blue). A snoball, however, is made with ice that is fluffy, soft like a Maine snowfall, and easily absorbs the cane-sugar syrup it gets soaked in.

Snoballs originated in New Orleans in the 1930s and remain a popular treat to beat the heat in Nola with stands all over the city. Lauren Gauthier, the founder of Little Easy Snoballs, spent her childhood in Southern Louisiana enjoying these snowy delights and was determined to bring her hometown favorite to the people of Maine.

You can usually find Little Easy Snoballs, an adorable, pint-sized green, yellow, and purple remodeled mail truck, parked in the Back Cove neighborhood of Portland. They are available for private events as well, which keeps them busy in the summer months, so it's best to check their social media to see where they'll be setting up shop during any given week.

Lauren's snoballs pack a punch with flavors including Wedding Cake, Lemon-Lime, Nectar, Watermelon, Grape and rotating flavors like Rosemary, Honey Lavender, Maine Blueberry, Basil, and Raspberry-Mint. And the fun doesn't stop there: you can opt to top off your snoball with ice cream, whipped cream, marshmallow fluff or condensed milk. They are piled high, and at first you might think there's no way you could possibly finish it—until you find yourself using a straw to suck up every last, refreshing sip from the bottom of the cup. Or at least that was my experience during my last visit with my piña colada/coconut/whipped cream dream.

It was after Lauren's move to Portland with her wife, Cassie, a Maine native, that she put her dream into action and brought Little Easy Snoballs to life. Maine is often described as being a boomerang state, a place that people grow up in, leave for a period of time, but often swoop back to after leaving the state to pursue work, school, and love. What gets pulled with them for the journey home, joining for the flight path back, are often new ideas cultivated during their growth outside the state and new ways to appreciate and contribute to their hometown. Cassie brought with her Lauren, and lucky for Maine, Little Easy Snoballs, a bit of Louisiana tradition. I love that Maine has that pull on people, a bottomless potion of staying power, allowing us to always be on the receiving end of new faces, new voices, new perspectives, and new backgrounds. Maine is hard not to miss and it's even easier to fall in love with. So, it serves as the perfect backdrop to pursue one half's dream project, in the other half's dream town.

While waiting for our snoballs, we watched Lauren hard at work inside the truck crafting her favorite treats while Cassie ran the register, entertaining guests as they perused the flavor options. One customer, delighted by the entire concept, asked Cassie how she got it up and running. "Oh, it was all her!" Cassie said, gesturing to her wife, a proud smile on her face, "Lauren figured out the permits, the logistics, all of it."

A Maine-based truck, with New Orleans' roots, running on love, nostalgia, and local pride.

Maine in Lauren's Words

A Favorite Maine Adventure

"We love living in Deering Center. Our typical Saturday morning entails heading out with our son and the dog to the trails at Baxter Woods, and then ordering a gooey butter cinnamon roll at Norimoto Bakery to eat together at Longfellow Elementary's playground. Outside of our neighborhood, we enjoy walking the La Verna Preserve in Bristol. It's an easy walk that ends with tide pools and an amazing coastal view. We of course always have to top it off with ice cream from Harbor Ice Cream."

Last Meal on Earth Somewhere in Maine

"It would definitely have to be the coq au vin at Chaval. It's meant for two, but I love it so much I tend to eat it all by myself. It's hard to want to share!"

A Person in Maine You Admire

"I'm inspired on a daily basis by Portland City Council member Victoria Pelletier. She's not even in my district, but I love how she synthesizes and makes city affairs accessible to the community and I feel as though I always know what's going on in Portland by following her. As a Black woman, it's also so refreshing to see Black female representation in Maine."

Why You Call Maine Home

"I followed my wife up here in 2019 after we lived together for 10 years in New Orleans. She comes from a big Maine family, and we wanted to start our own—our son was born in 2021. It's definitely been a big shift from growing up in Louisiana, but it's been great to be so close to amazing food, trails, and the coast, and we've also made awesome friends over the past three years. I can't wait to watch our son grow up here!"

....

Norimoto Bakery

Portland, Maine

Well, I had to try a gooey butter cinnamon roll. When I typed the Norimoto Bakery address into my GPS, I was sure I had it wrong. I'd passed that stretch on Stevens Avenue dozens of times before, and never noticed a bakery.

Sure enough, the bakery was indeed there, complete with a long line of pastry gawkers ogling the display case of the day's goodies. The bakery is understated. There is no formal sign out front, just a small, glowing "Hopeful" sign created by Maine-born artist Charlie Hewitt from his Hopeful Project beginning in 2019—what started as the artist's attempt to lift spirits during Maine's cold winters, now has installations across seven states at dozens of different sites.

Atsuko Fujimoto, the owner and James Beard-nominated baker, describes Norimoto Bakery's offerings as "European pastries with Japanese sensibility." Some of the offerings the day I visited included a pistachio visitandine with chocolate chips, a pluot almond danish, a jalapeño sausage roll and onigiri rice balls. Albeit difficult to do, I stuck to the plan and just ordered the cinnamon roll—however, almost every person in front of me stated their order and unanimously added: "actually, can I also get…" By the time they paid, they had doubled their orders, walking away with boxes full of goodies.

I ate the gooey butter cinnamon roll the second I got back in my car. It's fluffy, packed with cinnamon flavor, but is not overly sweet. It doesn't need a cinnamon roll's trademark cream cheese frosting—the softly sugared, delicate top is the perfect balance against the pillowy roll. I licked my fingers clean when

I finished and contemplated eating the other roll I had secured for Andrew. It was the best cinnamon roll I have ever had in my life—from a bakery hidden in plain sight.

Frenchman's Hole

Newry, Maine

"Where are you headed?" the cashier at the gas station asked, looking me up and down. My outfit was, admittedly, a bit disheveled, with tall hiking boots on, a bathing suit and cover-up on the top, and hair stuffed into a winter hat. I was prepared to let the day take me where it wanted to in Western Maine, part of my continued effort to go with the flow—even though that was still a cringeworthy idea to me, and executing it was still a challenge. Some hiking, maybe some swimming, a loose plan requiring outfit flexibility knowing that early summer in Maine is impossible to pin down, as far as weather is concerned. Chilly mornings can make way to humid afternoons.

"Frenchman's Hole," I began. "I'm writing a book." I then, much to her surprise and my own, erupted in laughter. She smiled back, unsure what the joke was. With trail mix in hand I continued to belly laugh all the way to my car.

This kept happening. Occasionally, when I was least expecting it, I would offer up to a stranger, unprompted, that I was writing a book and then immediately dissolve into a fit of giggles. Part of the laughter is surely a direct response to my imposter syndrome, maybe a touch of joy, but at the core of it, I think it's mostly in reaction to the freedom I am finding in not having to qualify it.

I have no precursor. I have no credentials, no magazine article to point to, no previous book on this topic to validate me. I'm not a travel writer, but I'm writing a book. It's hysterical to me—and so utterly freeing.

I arrived at the decision to write a book already well into my journey. My notes surrounding each adventure, each casual chat with a stranger, became more and more detailed, naturally weaving in and out of each other in story form, providing free therapy along the way. It's certainly not a novel idea to write about Maine; it's been done countless times before. I, however, have the distinct privilege of not having attached to it the crippling expectations that normally warp and smother everything I do.

It's not that I have never written before. I have. But each blog, article, or interview I completed as a college audition coach or actress held a suppressing amount of weight for me. If it was bad, or if I said the wrong thing or voiced the wrong opinion, my credibility might be smudged. I had a reputation to uphold, one that I had spent well over a decade honing. I've got nada here, zilch.

While it will come as no surprise to those who know me, I possess an uncanny ability to turn hobbies into jobs. Yet it feels incredibly powerful to choose to do something that brings me pleasure, without needing a label to back it up. I don't have to be a *New York Times* bestselling author to write a book that makes me feel good. Now if I could just tell that to people without the accompanying uproar of awkward laughter that stifles all responses and follow-up questions.

That wasn't happening on this day, however. My lingering chuckles finally subsided as I pulled onto the dirt road heading to the remote swimming hole nestled in the woods on Mahoosic public land. Being unpaved, the drive to Frenchman's Hole is pretty bumpy until you finally reach the parking lot. After parking, you walk back a bit the way you came and you'll find a simple stone staircase leading down to the waterfall and pool.

I expected to see a hoard of local teenagers, sliding into the freezing water using the natural rock water slide, pulling themselves back up with the rope secured along the right side of the gushing falls. The sun was out, the temperature rising steadily, the perfect weather for a dip. I imagined hearing happy screams coming from friends daring each other to take the plunge, holding hands as they submerged—you know, the type of stuff that provides great material for writing.

No one was there. Despite some cars in the parking lot, there wasn't one person at the swimming hole. Puzzled, I sat close to the water, getting splashed by the ten-foot tall plunge. I soon remembered it was a weekday in June, that fine line between the end of school and summer vacation, so most kids were still in their final stretch before camps and summer jobs kicked off.

Only a writer, sans any great writing material, here today I thought. I choked on my own laughter as I got ready for an afternoon swim.

IN SUNSCREEN

Quisisana Resort

Lovell, Maine

All of my worlds collide at Quisisana.

It's a place where my past and my present sing a duet, and where my story is inherently folded into the landscape. At Quisisana Resort, or "Quisi," on Lake Kezar in western Maine's White Mountains, the summer staff includes some of the brightest performing-arts students recruited from the top musical theater and acting programs in America. Many of them are my former students.

These performers are the heartbeat of Quisi, making up fifty percent of the staff. I heard one guest comment to her husband, "I'm not sure how they did it, but they somehow rounded up the nicest people in the world and employed them at this resort." With a grin, I thought, *This is a performer's speciality.* Artists are used to quickly, lovingly, and efficiently getting to know new people on a rotating basis. Performers, often employed on short contracts with new casts each time, are accustomed to forming close-knit, chosen-family bonds in a condensed period of time. You get really good at getting in deep, learning someone's inner workings, and connecting rapidly—only to say goodbye and start again a few months later. I often joked that I didn't have to try very hard to make friends as an actor—I was gifted new BFFs with the start of every show. My world was constantly expanding, my circle ever evolving.

With a family like this waiting to greet you at check-in, it's not surprising people return to Quisisana year after year—not just guests, but staff, too. Even for first timers, it felt like coming home.

Quisisana also takes "family friendly" to a level I have never before experienced at a resort, clinching it as one of my favorite getaways ever. Kids aren't an afterthought here, they are a celebrated, spoiled part of everything. There is a mini golf course on site, a playground, a building called Trebel Hall filled to the brim with toys, and a pristine swimming lake dotted with every sand toy you could imagine. Additionally, and perhaps most importantly for exhausted parents, every night (every night!) includes a dedicated kids' dinner followed by staffed playtime. This means you get to enjoy a peaceful, adult-only, sit-down dinner while your kiddo plays with their friends. Essentially, you get a full week of date nights with some of the finest food I have ever eaten at a resort.

But what makes Quisisana undeniably rare is its commitment to hire talented performers to put on nine different performances each week. These include chamber music, Broadway musicals, cabarets, a children's musical, and an opera. When they aren't onstage, the performers might serve you in the dining hall, get a boat ready for you, or babysit one of your children. Your mouth will be on the floor witnessing their

Quisisana Resort in Lovell, Maine.

breakout song in the evening show, and you'll be swimming in the lake together the following morning.

These are my people. Both the artists, who are experiencing the most ideal of summer gigs, and the guests, who are nature and Maine enthusiasts with a deep appreciation for the performing arts. I'm comfortable here—confident even. The ideal test audience to try out being more than one thing, or perhaps everything all at once, is here, nestled under the pine trees. Instead of running from the inevitable "What do you do?" question, or leading with the label I thought the person wanted me to be or seemed most impressive, what if I was everything simultaneously? What if I was equal parts momma, actress, hiker, writer, teacher, baker? Just me?

On my first evening at Quisi, while playing Go Fish with Harper on the deck at the Main Lodge, I grabbed a glass of wine from the bar to enjoy before dinner. When I gave my cottage name to the bartender for the bill, he responded with, "Oh, you're the travel writer!"

I froze for a second, expecting a round of giggles to surface, but instead I tried it on for size and simply said, "Yes, I am. Nice to meet you!"

I took selfies with our waiter to send to one of his best friends, a former student of mine. Listening to him talk about his next gig, an incredible opportunity in New York City, I told him I was so proud of him. I had known him for only a few minutes at that point, but I *was* proud. I knew getting that part would change his career. He was elated a guest understood the nuances of the business, and I was grateful to flex those muscles for the first time in a while.

I commiserated with another performer about the college audition process. She had auditioned for thirty-five programs, but I assured her this was normal. She blew bubbles with my daughter as we shared audition horror stories and our favorite local hikes.

Watching our daughters hold hands and jump into the moonlit lake in dresses, I laughed and connected with the mom of the little girl Harper adopted as her best friend for the week. This was our first extended trip with just the two of us and, honestly, I was proud of how well it was going. With no wifi in the cozy cedar cabins, we happily snuggled in to read chapter books every night, shared sit-down breakfasts and lunches where she used her best big-girl manners, built sand castles, and had swimming competitions to reach the dock. The fellow mom said that watching us together gave her the confidence to try something like this with just her daughter, too.

In the end, I stumbled my way through some conversations, but no one questioned my validity, or my ability to be the multiple characters that I cast myself as. I guess I'm the only one I need to convince.

The day we checked out, with a sad daughter in the backseat, I pulled out of the pine-needle-covered driveway passing Quisisana's outdoor theatre, reminiscing with Harper about the children's matinee performance of *Shrek* we saw there the day prior. While discussing her favorite characters, it suddenly dawned on me: I just, simply, watched it. I didn't anticipate the high notes in songs I knew like the back of my hand, I didn't think about costume changes, I didn't compare portrayals to those I had seen in the past. With some distance, and an attempt at authenticity on my part, the magic of theatre slowly crept back in and gave me a bear hug. I pulled out of Quisi rewarded with a renewed love of something that, as of late, completely fatigued me.

It's impossible to avoid being labeled. But I'm starting to make room on my shirt for multiple name tags.

Meet Rachel & Ryan Adams

Portland, Maine

@rachelgloriaia @ryanwritesonthings

To make the decision to pursue art full time is courageous, but to make the decision to pursue your art full time when you have young kids at home is monumental. It's a never-ending balancing act, a multiple-balls-in-the-air juggle of fostering your creative energy while carving out time for the little humans who rely on you. But if you figure out how to walk that tightrope, get really good at saying "yes" and "no," your balancing act becomes one that ultimately sets the stage for your kiddos' futures, a masterpiece highlighting what they themselves are also capable of.

It's something I never fully figured out while performing. I think there is a general lack of understanding or a compassion gap when it comes to being both a parent and an artist—ultimately requiring someone with untethered tenacity (or a very flexible support system) to do both successfully. I remember feeling scared and isolated when I started turning down auditions or gigs because I lacked childcare, or heading home early and missing an opening night party because I had a sick child at home or a babysitter that needed to be relieved. Time becomes an overwhelming theme: Should I take the time and plan the kid's dream vacation—risking having to say no to a valuable gig that will inevitably pop up? Should I use my sacred time after bedtime to memorize lines or just try to relax? Is the time spent on this project worth the time away from home?

On the flip side, with a shrinking of time comes a shrinking of overthinking: there's no time to waste to make it happen. Rachel and Ryan Adams, a Portland-based artist couple, are more than making it happen. Parents to two young girls, they are a tag-team support system, making sure they both get across that tightrope. I admire them because of their artistic contributions to Maine (and beyond) but I'm most impressed with their ability to make their girls a part—and often the intended audience—of those contributions. They trust the work, do it in the time they have allotted, all while knowing what their time is worth—to both themselves and their kids.

Their daughters get to enjoy two murals painted by their mom in the ever-awesome Children's Museum & Theatre of Maine. Rachel's blue-and-white mural is the backdrop to "Go with the Flow," while her bright red, orange-accented mural accompanies the "Ramp Up" exhibit. Any time the girls splash and play in the water tables, they get to soak up Mom's hard work behind them.

Spray painted murals throughout Maine, installed by Dad, are on display to proudly point out to friends. Geometric murals, Ryan's signature spray paint and latex gem designs, are featured at the Artist and Craftsman Supply store and Bissell Brothers Brewery, among so many others. His lettering and signage creations are noticeable while eating lunch at Highroller Lobster Co. or snacks and drinks at Novare Res. His time, his energy, his passion are on display, waiting for the girls to discover behind every corner.

But they aren't just painting what they want their girls to see, they are painting what they need them to see. Like Ryan's recent mural in Providence, "Stay Strong, Fight On"—created in the wake of the overturning of *Roe v. Wade.* It is a daily reminder for the public, of course, but a message for his young girls as well. His daughters were onsite while he completed that project.

And then there is the work they do for themselves. And in my opinion, it's one of the most vital parts of being an artist and a parent—you've got to take that time for *you* in order to turn it around and give it back to them. To turn off parent-mode for an hour or two, to put aside opportunity and business, and to give yourself room to create. I see this in Ryan's watercolors, I felt like I witnessed it in Rachel's installation titled "Joy" at The Press Hotel in Portland.

When I was attempting my own balancing act, Harper was too young to ever see me in a play. However, one night while snuggled up on the couch, I decided to play her a promotional video of a production I was currently in. She asked me to play it over and over, looking at me, back at the video, at me again. She hugged me, and in a moment of connecting the dots, processed what Mom does when she's away either performing or teaching. She said, "I love this."

Most children don't get the chance to really see what it is their parents do for work, to learn the source behind their occasional distractions, and to see what takes their favorite people away. Being an artist has its own unique set of ups and downs, a forever-shaky tightrope to walk, but what a gift that Rachel and Ryan's kiddos get to meet them on the other side. For them, and all of us, to witness and forever appreciate, their time spent on their artistic journey.

Maine in Rachel & Ryan's Words

A Favorite Maine Adventure

Rachel: "Oh my goodness, there are so many wonderful places in Maine! I love going to Rockland for their art and restaurant scene, Ferry Beach and Higgins Beach are the perfect family beach day locations, the shower at the spa at Inn by the Sea is worth every penny, and if I could live inside Chase's Daily in Belfast . . . I would. We live in Portland and it doesn't get much better than eating a BLVL (Belleville) pastry on a bench at the Eastern Prom or a ferry ride to Peaks Island. In our neighborhood we have Dear Dairy Ice Cream—on Fridays they scoop ice cream and behind the building is the most beautiful garden."

Ryan: "Wow, I have to agree with Rachel, there are SO many great places in this state. I'm born and raised here in Portland, so I'd be lying if I didn't profess my undying love for an Amato's Italian sandwich and/or pazzo bread. When I was in school in Boston, I would come home, see my folks, then go directly to Amato's. I have an Italian sandwich tattooed on me, so yeah, the love is strong. I also agree with Rachel with Inn By the Sea, and I would also add The Press Hotel. We stayed there on the night we got married, and we have continued to make it a stop annually ever since. The typography themed decor along with the history of the building and amazing views/cocktails hits all the points for me."

Last Meal on Earth Somewhere in Maine

Rachel: "Empire Chinese Kitchen: Hot and sour soup, har gow, green beans, and duck lo mein."

Ryan: "Scales: I'd have to go with the cloverleaf rolls, oysters, and the halibut. Words cannot describe…"

A Person in Maine You Admire

Rachel: "Sonya Tomlinson [Young Writers & Leaders Program Lead at The Telling Room]! I had the honor of mentoring through the Telling Room this past year and I have to say that Sonya Tomlinson's enthusiasm and respect for the kids in her program is quite special. She exudes joy and brings smiles to teenagers' faces from all over the world. She strengthens these kids' voices and helps give them confidence to be their authentic selves and share their stories. She's amazing."

Ryan: "Jordan Carey and Madison Poitrast-Upton of Loquat. They are young and innovative POCs that have a clothing and textile design company downtown in Portland. They bring a fresh and inspiring style and flavor to the town, and they are undeniably talented. I love following along and watching them succeed."

Why You Call Maine Home

Rachel: "I don't want to speak ill of my home state of Massachusetts but when I moved to Portland in 2005 it felt like I had finally found a place I belonged. The people, the food, the accessibility to the coast and mountains. Portland felt like a hub of outsiders, an awkward mix of creative humans. It's hard to imagine my life outside of Portland."

Ryan: "I was born and raised here, and I absolutely love it. Portland has changed quite a bit over the past few years, and I have unfortunately seen some things that I loved about this small city/big town go. But there have also been so many wonderful things that have arrived as a result of the growth. I love that I can drive twenty minutes in any direction and be in the most beautiful and serene locations in the woods, on the beach, or on a lake. I also love that it is safe and that the community is very strong here. It makes me excited and happy to be able to raise my kids in such a wonderful place."

••

Loquat

Portland, Maine

Founded by MECA graduates Jordan Carey and Madison Poitrast-Upton, Loquat empowers marginalized people and causes through fashion and design. Their space is filled with collaborations and contributions from BIPOC, LGBTQ+, disabled, and chronically ill artists and entrepreneurs.

From clothing to sturdy bags to plant propagators and tiny knickknacks, you'll have no problem finding a perfect gift—for someone else or yourself. I purchased a pair of stunning, locally made earrings from Studio Choo11, based in Scarborough, that haven't left my ears since.

The petite store is tucked into the bottom level of the building at 58 Exchange Street in Portland. As such, it can be unknowingly passed by in the midst of a busy Old Port afternoon. But once you find it, you'll never pass by without popping in again.

Goss Berry Farm

Mechanic Falls, Maine

Strawberry picking gets a lot of love in Maine. It's pretty much one of our seasons. When that sweet spot of peak strawberry season arrives, usually right around the middle of June, you'll notice local restaurants offering strawberry-themed recipes from their favorite picking spots, social media will fill with images of overflowing strawberries in green baskets, and our mouths and fingers become stained a soft red.

It's a tradition in our house, too. But this year, we decided to switch it up and not only try a new picking spot, but also a different type of berry, with a different peak timeline. We're wild.

Endless rows of raspberry and blueberry bushes can be found at Goss Berry Farm in Mechanic Falls, just west of Lewiston. There are so many rows that you will likely have a whole section to yourself to pick and never run into another person. We pretended we were in the live action version of *Blueberries for Sal*, kerplunking until our baskets were filled to the brim. The blueberries were a luscious deep blue color with a dusting of gray on the surface; the raspberries a rich, vibrant red. Now that

I have seen (and tasted) what they are like straight off the bush, it'll be hard to go back to store bought.

Looking as if Harper had put a fresh coat of red lipstick on, we opted to pay more in the "guilt jar" at the end—a place to make amends for the snacking along the route. Consciences wiped clean, we munched on fresh berries all the way home.

Bresca & The Honey Bee at Outlet Beach

New Gloucester, Maine

I'd pretty much follow chef Krista Kern Desjarlais, a James Beard Award finalist who has had a long and varied career in Maine, anywhere that she decides to serve her food and desserts. And when her natural, inventive ice cream happens to be at a quaint swimming hole where you can spend an entire day swimming, floating, and connecting with your family, even better.

For a small fee, you can set up shop at Outlet Beach on Sabbathday Lake—a traditional swimming hole that is shallow enough for the youngest of the littles to safely play and swim without worry. Harper is not the most confident swimmer, but it was here that I watched her bravely grab a swimming tube and make her way to the floating dock without me in tow. She occasionally turned her head to make sure that I was where she left me, but once my location was confirmed, she continued her little leg kicks to shadow the big kids around her.

When she made her way back to the beach, the joy she felt from my praise was quickly overshadowed by a scoop of birthday cake sprinkle ice cream from the shack. I rewarded my supreme parenting with a scoop of crème fraîche key lime pie.

Sticky and full, we ran back down to the beach to give the waterslide a try.

Intervale Pizza & Village Store

New Gloucester, Maine

I wasn't kidding about following Krista Kern Desjarlais wherever she decides to serve her ice cream. Add her husband, the talented Erik Desjarlais, to the list as well.

After a long hike in New Gloucester, I promised my tired family pizza. I had heard about a pizza joint inside of a village market only a few minutes away, so we scooted over. From the outside, it appears to be your typical, local market but when you walk in, you are instantly hit with the unmistakable smell of a wood-fired pizza oven. We scanned the menu quickly, taking note of choices ranging from your standard cheese to the wicked hot (Calabrian chilis, pickled red onions, scallions, and ricotta) and more adventurous picks like the pickle & sausage (sausage, pickles, roasted onions, and white sauce.) Being ravenous, indecisive, and supremely excited—we ordered three pizzas for the three of us. As you do. The pies arrived—classic cheese for the little lady, pepperoni for my hubby and the broccoli for me (garlic ricotta cream, broccoli, sweet roasted onions, and cheddar).

We made a unanimous decision: this was some of the best pizza we've ever had in Maine. As we headed to the door, despite being very full, I had to peek into the ice cream freezer. To my delight, the freezer was packed full of Bresca and the Honeybee's creamy ice cream, touting flavors like rhubarb, buttermilk panna cotta and bergamot ricerelli.

After later learning who was behind the establishment, I wasn't surprised in the slightest. As this talented duo has shown us time and time again with their contributions to Maine's food scene, if you build it—with love, integrity and unconventional character—they will come.

Unfortunately, in September 2023, The Intervale Pizza and Village Market hung up their pizza peel for the last time, citing a series of obstacles that had piled up. While I'm sad to say you won't be able to try their addictive pizza, I don't think you'll have to wait long to witness whatever comes next from this gifted cook.

Meet Karl Thomsen

Jackman, Maine

On my eighth attempt at calling Karl, he finally answered. Karl, whose title ranges from Lakeside Guardian to Dock Master for Attean Lake Lodge, a twenty-four-acre island in Jackman featuring all-inclusive cabin rentals, has never owned a cell phone. The resort provides him with one during the summer so they can reach him from across the lake, but he is by no means tied to it. In fact, he avoids it altogether after noontime because that is when the telemarketers usually try to reach him. Karl also has no email address, no social media, and no computer. He has successfully avoided them entirely for all of his sixty-two years. Getting in touch with Karl is difficult—just the way he likes it.

Depending on the study you read, Americans check their phones between one hundred and more than three hundred times per day. It's an addiction that we collectively know is wrong and shameful, but we do it anyway. Imagine not only eliminating, but never introducing, our dopamine dealer and depletor.

"Life is so much easier my way, I find," Karl began, "I often hear guests say they want to throw their phones in the lake." In Karl's world, there is no Facebook. There are no group texts, no likes or emojis, he never received a classic chain email from the late nineties, never suffered through a Tiktok dance video. "I like my own company," Karl tells me. "I read a lot. I entertain myself. I laugh at myself a lot, actually." And if you've ever met Karl, you'd have to agree—he is more entertaining and has stories significantly more meaningful than any movie or television series.

While employed with the resort during the summer, Karl can be found in a small cabin without electricity at the landing of Attean Lake, greeting guests after they park. As soon as Karl hears your tires pull into the dirt lot, he'll emerge to help load your belongings onto the boat that will then escort you to the island. While waiting for the boat to dock, Karl will amuse you with stories about the resident dog that roams the resort and give you tips on sleeping the first night if you aren't accustomed to total, utter, beautiful silence. And once on your way, with a wave goodbye, Karl will disappear back into the solace of his own company.

There's a comfort in knowing Karl will be there when we visit in the summer; it's a sort of old-school nostalgia, meeting at an agreed upon place at a set time. He guides moose hunts in the fall, partakes in his own deer hunts in the winter, shovels some snow and keeps the water running for a local campground—and then the summer is back again, where he'll meet you at Attean, with new stories to share.

....

Maine in Karl's Words

A Favorite Maine Adventure

"I used to guide whitewater rafting and those were some of my favorite times. I enjoyed doing the overnight trips, making people happy, camping in the woods, feeding them well. It's nice to take someone from the city and help them have a good time without any of their stuff from home. They realize that a few days in the woods without their amenities is actually kind of neat."

Last Meal on Earth Somewhere in Maine

"It'd be a frying pan full of six to eight inch brook trout with fried potatoes. You can find them in little streams or bogs; they are bright orange. They aren't a lake or pond fish. That's my favorite meal—some brook trout from any little stream in Maine."

A Person in Maine You Admire

"A friend of mine in Aroostook County. His name is Preston Bonney and his father is a retired game warden. I learned an awful lot about the woods from that man. He's quiet—and lives with the woods. I'm like him: he's taught me to be comfortable in the woods with next to nothing—that you are better off with less."

Why You Call Maine Home

"It's got everything I need, really. I hunt, fish, trap—my whole life revolves around the woods. Any place that has some good woods, that's where you'll find me—and when I say woods, I mean a couple hours off the trail. I can just be me there."

Attean Lake Lodge

Jackman, Maine

Guests at Attean Lake Lodge, a former camp founded in the 1890s on Birch Island, must take a page out of Karl Thomsen's book—if only for a long weekend stay. Each wooden cabin is equipped with a bathroom and hot water, but no electricity and no wifi. With the exception of the Main Lodge, there is no cell service, and you are encouraged to leave phones in your rustic cabin for the duration of your stay.

On our first visit, after unpacking and some obligatory bed jumping for Harper, I watched Andrew check his phone and clock that his emails weren't coming through. With some hesitation, he exhaled and placed his phone on the bedside table where it remained for the weekend. Instead of doom scrolling, we competed in a few rounds of checkers while our daughter

Attean Lake Lodge in Jackman, Maine.

played in the fully stocked kids' game room. Turns out there really wasn't anything all that important to attend to back in the real world.

After a hearty dinner each night (included with your stay), we usually run down to the beach to catch the sunset. Harper likes to build sand castles or play with Dakota—the gigantic island dog and family pup of Attean Lake Lodge owners Jocelyn and Barrett Holden. Andrew and I find a place on the dock, dip our toes in the water, and watch the sky change.

At breakfast, Harper usually enjoys her standard order of fresh blueberry pancakes and we alternate between stuffed omelets or waffles. It's there we grab our lunch for the day—a simple sandwich, chips, fruit and a canteen filled with lemonade. The packed lunch encourages guests to get off their regular schedules and see where the day takes them.

Our days at Attean are spent kayaking, hiking nearby mountains accessible by boat, pursuing sunrise self-guided moose searches, and best of all, doing nothing at all. We cycle through books, family naps, and beers on the deck. We have the occasional cannonball contest off the dock, share ghost stories over kerosene lamps at night, and play hide and seek around the island.

Attean Lake Lodge has become Harper's benchmark of what a family trip should be. She has her parents completely uninterrupted, fully engaged, and relaxed. Her happy place is an island in the center of Attean Lake, the one guarded by Karl, where wifi doesn't quite reach.

Little Hunter's Beach

Mount Desert Island, Maine

I'm not one of those people who loves when it rains. However, I very much love the hour directly following a rainfall. The type of weather that makes your hair instantly curl as a gentle fog hovers and surfaces remain slick. It was during one of these peaceful, misty hours we experienced an extremely rare moment during peak Acadia National Park season—July, gasp—my family and I were the only souls on the beach. The clouds looked angry still, keeping the crowds at bay, and the hazy, tranquil beach was all ours. Little Hunter's Beach, west of Otter Point, sits along the south-facing coastline of Mount Desert Island. It is made up of cobblestones of every size and color.

This little oasis is just a few steps away from the busy Park Loop Road, but if you didn't know it was there, you'd never pull over, as it's not listed on Acadia's maps. A dramatic, wooden staircase will wind you down to the stunning beach tucked within a small cove. This isn't a swimming beach, or a traditional Acadia hike. It's a quick stop to stroll, do some pondering, and mosey along. On our visit this year, as if Harper knew the silent serenity we stumbled upon, she sat quietly tucked under my arm watching the waves crash for a whole ten minutes—a new record.

Little Hunter's Beach on Mount Desert Island.

Beech Mountain

Southwest Harbor, Maine

If you've ever wanted to feel like you were on the set of *Jurassic Park* or *Lord of the Rings,* there's a trail in Southwest Harbor that will do the trick. Beech Mountain is a popular trail, but most folks only pursue the short 1.2-mile Beech Mountain Loop Trail to reach the fire tower at the summit in a quick, sweaty manner. Valid enough, but if you only pursue this loop, you'll miss the chance to see huge, moss-covered, fallen boulders—and maybe a hobbit or dinosaur—on the alternate route to the summit, the Valley Trail.

Covered in roots and lined with spruce, the dark, forested valley beneath Beech Mountain feels cloaked in mystery. If I were a troll or fairy, you better believe this is where I would set up shop. After looking behind the massive stones and peering into every mossy crevice, you'll eventually hit the Beech South Ridge Trail to bring you to the top of the mountain. Climbing atop the fire tower at the summit, you can take in views of Long Pond, Echo Lake, the Atlantic Ocean, and the western side of Mount Desert Island. For your best chance to see something whimsical, I'd recommend the following two-mile route:

Up Valley Trail (.8 mile)
continue up Beech South Ridge Trail (.8 mile)
and come down Beech Mountain Trail (.4 mile)

Anemone Cave at Schooner Head Overlook

Bar Harbor, Maine

You won't find Anemone Cave, an ancient sea cave, on the usual Acadia National Park maps either. There are no signs, clear paths, or other markings to direct you to it. In fact, after parking at the Schooner Head Overlook, as you head toward the water and begin your walk along the rocky coast, you won't even know that you are standing directly on top of the cave. That wasn't always the case; it used to be one of the major attractions within the park.

There are a few reasons the crowds are no longer directed here. For one, it's dangerous. The cave is only accessible at low tide and if you attempt to head here at high tide, the cave will be completely submerged. The risk of drowning as the water comes in is very real. Additionally, the rocks within the sea cave are outrageously slick. Many rocks are completely covered in seaweed, and the ones that look like they might be okay are deceptively very slippery as well. Shoes with good traction, common sense, and a slow, deliberate pace over the stones is essential.

But humans present danger here as well. There are delicate, fragile sea creatures living in the incredibly beautiful tidal pools that reveal themselves when the tide goes out. Bright pink seaweed, hundreds of periwinkles, dark red anemone, green crabs, and bright orange starfish relax in the pools. Touching them, moving them about and manipulating their environment is harmful to these creatures—and enough to get the cave stripped from the park maps.

However, if you are equipped with this knowledge, and treat the cave (and yourself) with care, it's an experience that will never leave you. The fifteen minutes we spent exploring, seeing starfish for the first time ever in the wild, and watching the ocean twinkle in the distance from within the damp, dark cave, will be a memory forever etched within the three of us.

40 Miles of the Solar System

Presque Isle, Maine

The sky looked as if it was going to swallow us whole. My heart was pounding as we cruised along Route 1 in Presque Isle, watching the sky shift from dark blue to stormy black, threatening to erupt at any second. As we slowed passing Saturn, the fourth planet in the forty miles of the solar system heading north on the famed road through Aroostook County, we heard a boom of thunder.

This Maine Solar System Model recreates the respective distances between the sun and planets along a stretch of highway. Constructed by the University of Maine at Presque Isle in 2000, it's the fourth largest scale model solar system in the world. Some of the planets, like Pluto and Mercury, are placed inside information centers or stationed on University of Maine Presque Isle's campus, making them impossible to spot from the road during an impending thunderstorm. However, I had bookmarked Saturn, Jupiter, and Mars to use as distractions to keep Harper entertained as we drove through the rolling landscape of northern Maine right beside the border of Canada.

Upon reaching Jupiter, located a little more than five miles from the sun, a light drizzle began to hit our windshield. Even from the road and through rainy windows, this giant gas planet's trademark red and orange strokes were visible. An impressive amount of artistic detail is visible from the road.

Don't blink (especially in a thunderstorm) or you'll miss Mars. Located directly next to the Presque Isle welcome sign, it's a mile and a half from the sun. After a quick squint from the side of the road to view the second smallest planet in our solar system, a massive lightning bolt lit up the sky to our left. And then the rain began pelting our car.

I pulled off to the side of the road, unable to see even a foot in front of us. A rush of thunder echoed throughout the expansive fields to our right and the ground seemed to shake our car. I did my best to comfort our scared little one in the backseat, but frankly, I was scared, too. We only had three miles to go to reach our AirBnB, and with the rain letting up slightly, Andrew took over the driving while I took some big breaths in the passenger seat. Cracked, fallen trees were scattered along the road, and police cars with flashing lights surrounded the wreckage. Broken fences and belongings cluttered people's yards. It looked like a tornado had whipped through the County.

We fumbled with the security box but managed to open the AirBnB's front door before getting too soaked. Once inside, I promptly poured myself a gigantic glass of red wine and set up shop on the couch. The rain eventually subsided, but with nerves shot, we weren't going anywhere tonight. With a full day ahead of us tomorrow, I went to bed shortly after Harper.

I felt a gentle pat around eleven that night. I shot up, clearly still anxious from hours prior, to find Andrew motioning for me to go outside. Resigned to find a tree on top of our car, or a broken window, I hurried to take a look. "You have to see this," he said, as I exited the house.

A bright blanket of innumerable stars lit up the sky, along with thousands of fireflies twinkling in the sunflower fields and blossoming potato fields surrounding us. Aroostook County is so lightly populated, so much more free of artificial light from towering buildings, street lights, and cars than other parts of Maine, that when you look up at the night sky it's as if you are in your own personal planetarium. I tilted my head to the stars, twirling my body around and around, watching stars flicker in and out while tracing the Big Dipper and Little Dipper with my fingers. From the ground up, we were in a sparkly wonderland.

"I wish Harper was awake to see this," Andrew said. We caught eyes, beelined to her bedroom and grabbed a big blanket to wrap her in. As we exited the house, her head resting on her Dad's shoulders, she rubbed her sleepy eyes and caught her first glimpse of the lightning bugs floating around her. If she had ever seen them before, which I don't recall, she had certainly never seen them in these numbers. She woke up to a type of magic that she only reads about in her favorite, fantasy-filled bedtime books.

Tucked in tightly to Andrew, she was mostly silent as we twirled, taking in the night. Just before heading back inside, I watched her eyes widen, remembering something.

"Saturn, Jupiter, and Mars are up there," she said.

Meet Olivia Hammond

Blaine, Maine
@doublegfarms1, @foxfamilychips

There's no lack of potatoes in Aroostook County. On any major road in the Crown of Maine, during mid-July through October, you'll pass a plethora of roadside stands with hand-painted signs boasting "New Potatoes." New potatoes, which are small potatoes dug from Aroostook soil early in the season, have a skin so delicate you don't need to peel them. The honor-system stands will be filled to the brim with these new potatoes—along with their more mature potato siblings—offering five and ten pound bags for just a couple of dollars. There are acres upon acres of potato fields sprawling in every direction.

You might take these spuds for granted and maybe not appreciate how they landed on your dinner plate, when you are in the presence of so many. You could have counted me in that pool—until, that is, I watched a video of Maine's potato harvest season. During harvest, farmers typically spend a condensed four weeks working up to twelve-hour days, which start before the sun comes up. They end their days covered in dust and grime from head to toe. One farm during this period might harvest well over twenty million individual potatoes. And this is just their work during harvest season—the four-week hustle after a year of preparing, caring for, and agonizing over this year's crops.

What also can be found during harvest are local Aroostook County students on their annual potato harvest school break, during which they learn how to spot bad potatoes on a conveyor belt and build a strong work ethic. A longstanding tradition, often known as simply "the harvest" or "potato recess," this break yields these students a paycheck at the end of the week, appreciation for the agriculture in their town, and the immense gratitude from the farmers in need of the help.

Double G Farms is a family business run by Gregg Garrison and his children, Spencer Garrison and Olivia (Garrison) Hammond. Gregg's father, Wayne Garrison, purchased his first thirty acres in Blaine in 1965. When Gregg graduated college in 1988, he joined his family back at the farm and Double G Farms was born. They grow potatoes for Pineland Farms, McCain Foods, Penobscot McCrum, and Fox Family Chips. In 2013, Double G Farms partnered with Fox Family Chips to form Trinity Chips, LLC, allowing the farm to be the sole provider of quality russets to be used for the one-hundred-percent Maine potato chip company.

Olivia has become the unofficial spokesperson for both brands. After hearing stories of her love of the farm, of her neighbors and the place she's always called home—it's obvious enough why they point to Olivia when questions need answering. She's extraordinarily hard working and has a deep connection to her land and an unwavering commitment to her community. She's a kindhearted, tried-and-true Mainer whose family is, and will likely always be, inherently folded into the landscape. She's the perfect Mainer to emulate, if you're from away, like I am.

Maine in Olivia's Words

A Favorite Maine Adventure

"My favorite place to visit in Maine is the New England Outdoor Center on Millinocket Lake. It's right on the water with a beautiful view of Mount Katahdin. My family has been going there every summer for the last seven years. The area is so peaceful. I love taking a kayak out on the water and watching the sunset on the other side of the mountain. It almost feels like time stands still when you're out on the water there. I also have had the opportunity to climb Mount Katahdin three times. Although it is very challenging, the hike is worth it for the amazing views. It is quite something that we have such a beautiful mountain and area right here in Maine. I hope to be able to climb the mountain many more times over the years."

Last Meal on Earth Somewhere in Maine

"If I had to choose my last meal on Earth from a restaurant in Maine I would choose the Downunder in Houlton. They have the best nachos that I have ever had!"

A Person in Maine You Admire

"A person that I admire in Maine is Rhett Fox. About twenty years ago he had a dream to start a potato-chip company and now it has grown into a very successful business. Over the years I've had a front row seat to see just how hard Rhett works every day to do what he loves. I've seen Rhett put in countless hours at the Fox Family Chip plant and on the road delivering chips and meeting with customers. I hope to someday have the same drive and determination that Rhett has."

Why You Call Maine Home

"I call Maine home because it is a beautiful area to live and raise a family. Aroostook County has some of the most beautiful sunrises and sunsets I've ever seen. I also call Maine home because of my job. I grew up on my family's potato farm and I now get to raise my kids doing the same thing that I did with my parents on the farm."

....

Fox Family Chips

Mapleton, Maine

We pulled up to the chip plant to find Rhett Fox waiting for us outside. He welcomed us with a wave and, before addressing Andrew or I, knelt down to Harper's eye level and asked her if she liked chips. She gave an enthusiastic nod. You know a fellow parent when you meet one—there's an unmistakable generosity and patience emanating from them—and out of the many roles Rhett plays, I bet dad is one of his favorites.

If a sandwich shop carries Fox Family Chips, I'm confident I am going to love my lunch. Forget the turkey sandwich; it's really just an excuse to rip open a bag of my favorite potato chips. I'm partial to the salt and vinegar flavor, but plain and BBQ run a close second. I'm in a committed, monogamous relationship with these sturdy, crave-worthy chips. So when given an invitation to visit the modest chip plant stationed in Mapleton, not open to the public as many of my other adventures are, I jumped at the chance.

When you enter the chip plant, it smells like you have stepped inside of a baked potato. A salty, savory aroma hangs in the air as the potatoes are hustled through every stage in the process—cleaning, cutting, frying, and bagging in a harmonious manner. The potatoes, freshly delivered from Double G Farms, circled all around us as they moved through the process, ultimately filling the unmistakable silver bags at the end of the line. "My kids drew the logo," Rhett began, showing off the hand drawn foxes adorning the front of the bag. "People thought I should make it more professional, but I said no way."

Born into a family of potato farmers, Rhett began experimenting with creating the perfect potato chip in the late 1990s. He'd slice them by hand using a meat slicer and fry them in a mixture of canola and corn oil to reach his desired color. Just as when it first began, Fox Family Potato Chips remains trans-fat free with no artificial colors, ingredients, or preservatives. They taste like a locally sourced Maine potato in bite size, crunchy form—probably because that's exactly what they are.

"Have you ever had a warm potato chip?" Rhett asked Harper toward the end of the tour. She shook her head—and although we weren't asked, we shook our head side to side as well, hoping we also might get a hot chip. Instead of handing just a couple to Harper, he emerged with three gigantic bags filled with freshly fried, piping hot chips. He handed each of us our own bag, enough to accompany my turkey sandwiches for the rest of the month, and warned us that once we tried a warm chip, we'd be ruined for life. When we finally left, hands greasy and with salty lips, we had to pry Harper's hands out of her bag. If you are ever offered a freshly fried potato chip, I suggest you take it, though you have been warned.

We sat outside with Rhett in his "summer office," a picnic table resting along the edge of the chip plant, before getting back on the road. He shared stories of growing up in northern Maine, the inevitable ups and downs of running a family business, and his joy in raising his kids here surrounded by kind neighbors.

"It's the people," Rhett began. "Because it can be hard to make a living up here, but there is no better place to raise your family."

Rhett's people, his chosen and biological family, are what continue to replenish and fuel him to follow a dream he had twenty years ago. It's not just the name of the business; it's the reason.

Buck Farms & Maine Malt House

Mapleton, Maine

I didn't understand half of the things Caleb Buck showed me on our tour of the Maine Malt House, a large-scale operation that expertly malts grains. If I'm being honest, probably more than half. And that's not because Caleb isn't an excellent tour guide—he's thorough, extremely detailed, and patient—it's just that what the four Buck Brothers are doing on their multi-generational family farm, with their own unique process and machinery, is extremely nuanced and high tech. From their floor malting system to their state-of-the-art grain cleaning and processing equipment to the intricate computer software systems that streamline workflow, every square inch of their facility is maximized for efficiency. Caleb essentially led us through a chemistry lesson, a whirlwind of scientific study from someone who is, essentially, self taught. The amount of work that goes into cultivating quality local malt is utterly dizzying.

But let's bring it back to the basics for a second (and also the first question I asked Caleb after he painstakingly went through their entire process): What is malt? Malt is grain that has been modified through steeping, germination, and kilning to be in primo shape for brewing, distilling, etc. It's vital for beer because it is what provides the alcohol content—plus the mouth-feel, head, color, and flavor.

Lucky for the Buck Brothers (Jared, Joshua, Jacob, and Caleb), the number of breweries per capita in Maine is one of the highest in the country. And it was after a tour of a Maine brewery that the idea materialized for the brothers to provide locally malted barley for our ever-evolving craft beer scene so that breweries could source their malt in-state. This was after toying with the idea of producing beets, among other potential crops, once it became clear their family's farm could no longer support the next generation with work unless there was an expansion in their products.

In 1958, Caleb's grandfather, Jack, planted his first crops of potatoes on a forty-acre field in northern Maine. These crops that would help cultivate and inspire the next generations of farmers within his family. Buck Farms has since grown to 1,700 acres and transitioned from potatoes to quality grains, oil seeds, and legumes—with, of course, the huge addition being the Maine Malt House pumping out exceptional local malt.

When I asked Caleb for a tour of the facility, I was not expecting him to take the time with us that he did. We got to hang out with Caleb for more than an hour, touring both the Maine Malt House and other crops on the property (including their remarkable bright yellow rows of mustard). The majority of his extended family either lives directly on the property, or just a few minutes down the road, and as we neared the end of our tour, Caleb's grandmother greeted us just outside her home. She had no idea who we were, but that didn't matter, we knew Caleb somehow and that was enough for her. She regarded us like we were relatives, treating Harper as though she was one of her own precious grandkids. We felt wrapped in her warmth, despite being total strangers.

Our time in Aroostook County was short, but even during our condensed trip, it was so abundantly clear through every interaction how much The County's people are getting it right, this whole life thing. The Buck Brothers listened to what their state needed, came up with a solution, worked tirelessly to become the very best at it—all while getting to hang out with each other in the process. They get to move through life and business together, with visits to Grandma throughout.

Frye Island

Frye Island, Maine

The lack of information surrounding Frye Island, a 1,500-acre island in the middle of Sebago Lake, made it all the more intriguing to visit. After some digging, I found only two articles circulating on the internet about the summer community, each one offering a glimpse into life on the island, but both with details missing. After I visited the island, however, I think this might be intentional.

Residents make their way to Frye Island from May to October, vacating it the rest of the year when the water is shut off. The island is accessed by a cash-only public car ferry, departing every twenty to thirty minutes in the summer. The ride across the lake takes less than ten minutes, and you stay in your car for the trip. At first, I was hesitant to take the car ferry as I'd much prefer to walk or bike my way around the island, if possible. However, once I got my first glimpse of the twenty-two miles of dirt roads that criss-cross throughout the island, it was obvious a golf cart or car is the best mode of transportation.

Sebago Lake, the second largest in Maine at forty-five square miles, is deep, clean, and made for summer swimming. And Frye Island makes it easy for its residents and guests to enjoy this gem with thirteen sandy beaches to choose from. We set up shop at Beach #6, a lagoon-esque beach featuring a six-foot-tall lighthouse. When we asked locals which beach they preferred, each person gave a different answer, citing their reasons. Some grappled with the answer, finding it tough to choose just one—a wonderful dilemma, to be sure.

In addition to the beaches, there is a nine-hole golf course in the center of the island, a community center, and a restaurant with a general store attached. Frye's Leap Cafe, situated directly on the lake, bustles with patrons for lunch and dinner. We snagged a table for lunch, were accompanied by some local ducks hoping for scraps, and munched our sandwiches while watching boats and jet skis whip by. Naturally, I also enjoyed a Frye's Leap IPA, a hoppy, medium-bodied beer brewed by Sebago Brewing.

Our waitress, a teenager who has spent the majority of her summers on the island, was happy to have finally landed the coveted position as server. Most kids on the island start as ice-cream scoopers at the stand attached to the general store, eventually moving up through the various kitchen and store responsibilities. The island also prides itself on being mostly run by volunteers. It is a community that manages itself, from ice-cream scooper to ferry operator.

Because there are fewer than five hundred homes, most folks know each other by first name. It's a quiet paradise that likes to keep a low profile. Some Maine islands along the coast cater to summer tourists, but, while Frye Island does offer amenities open to both familiar faces and ferry hoppers with short-term stays, don't expect a red carpet. No posters promoting island services or flashy advertisements about guided tours can be found. It's an island for simple, timeless fun where the goal of any visitor should be to blend in, make memories, and tip well.

Nervous Nellie's Jams & Jellies

Deer Isle, Maine

Nervous Nellie's makes more than three hundred jars of jam a day by hand. Their flavors include wild blackberry peach conserve, strawberry rhubarb, Maine blueberry, hot tomato chutney, and Sunshine Road marmalade, among many others. The flavors alone are intriguing enough to add it to your itinerary when visiting Downeast Maine, but you are in for a world of surprise if you think you're just quickly stopping at a roadside store, on a bridged Maine island, for some authentic Maine-made jelly.

The grounds at Nervous Nellie's Jams and Jellies are a truly lifelong, ever-evolving work in progress by husband-and-wife team Anne and Peter Beerits. Peter, a sculptor specializing in using upcycled, discarded metal, lumber, and other found material, has scattered his masterpieces throughout the six-acre property. Upon entering the fantasyland, you'll first walk directly into Nellieville—a life-sized, western town replica that includes a jail, a saloon, a lawyer's office, and a hotel. You can enter each building, say hello to the patrons at the bar, pretend to get a reading from the fortune teller upstairs, and create your own story using the intricately decorated sculptures from Peter's imagination. Venture further into the property and you'll find a large trail through the woods that houses a multi-story wizard's tower, a church, a general store, and a 1950s garage where a few sculptures are having a jam session (with guitars, that is, not a sandwich making party.)

After all that exploring, you can pick up that jar of jam you came for, plus other locally made goodies, in their gift shop. Visitors are allowed to explore the grounds during operating hours on Tuesdays through Saturdays from mid-May through October.

Frinklepod Farm

Arundel, Maine

Pssst! I know how to drastically brighten or improve your day—a one-stop shop to lift your spirits and fill that happiness tank.

Get thee to flower picking at Frinklepod Farm! The farm provides the scissors, vases, and rows of flowers—all you need to do is bring your vision. Within the flower fields you'll find blooms like zinnias, celosia, sunflowers and unique finds like love-in-a-mist and sea holly. From early July through late September, the Pick-Your-Own Flower Patch is open Wednesdays through Sundays during their normal business hours.

Frinklepod is a small, family-owned, certified organic farm in Arundel, not far from Kennebunkport, that grows vegetables, fruits, herbs, and flowers. When paying for your floral harvest, you can feel good about any other goodies you grab in the store—Frinklepod Farm supports the local food economy by carrying products made by other local producers in addition to their own.

Horse Island Camp

Peaks Island, Maine

For two weeks in the summer, Harper participated in Horse Island Camp on Peaks Island. Founded in 1998, Horse Island Camp teaches young campers how to properly groom, saddle, and ride horses all while instilling in them the importance of treating these animals with kindness. When I picked her up each day, Harper was covered in mud from head to toe—a sure sign of a summer day well spent.

Getting to Horse Island Camp, however, is quite the experience. To register for camp, you must complete a paper application and mail a check to the owner, Jeanie. You won't receive a confirmation if you have nabbed a spot. In fact, your only communication before camp starts is in the form of a voided check if they didn't have a spot for your kiddo. A printed paper application with an attached check feels slightly archaic, and yet, it somehow feels just right for this camp.

Each morning, campers take the morning ferry over to Peaks from Portland with the rest of their animal-loving pals and a scattering of counselors. The ferry ride is just fifteen minutes, enough time to play some simple name games and share random horse facts among the group. Once the boat docks, campers walk a mile to the center of the island where the horses and camp are located. Half-day campers can be picked up at the campground at lunchtime; full-day kids walk the mile back to the ferry, to meet their parents in Portland just after five. No matter how you shake it, kids take two boat rides, walk two miles, and spend their days in the sun, playing in fields with horses. It's a lot—and they all adore it.

Harper was a half-day camper, so I took the ferry with her each day to explore Peaks before pick-up time. Some days I would set up in a coffee shop to document some recent adventures, other days I'd pack lightly and spend the morning playing tourist, traipsing through the town and its tree-lined streets. After two weeks on the island (which is just three miles from downtown Portland), I began to recognize faces, became part of the morning mix and routine, watched ferries unload with peppy crowds, walked every paved and dirt road, and formed a much deeper love of Peaks.

Baba's Cafe

Peaks Island, Maine

I'd hug Harper goodbye for Horse Camp and make a beeline to Baba's for an iced coffee, or if feeling wild, an iced americano. This espresso bar and bakery opened in 2022, but judging from the long line spilling out from the register down its front steps, you'd think they had already secured a full docket of regulars. It's just a three-minute walk from the ferry and you'd be making a mistake if you didn't grab their breakfast sandwich. In addition to their daily mix of pastries, they have only one breakfast sandwich—but if you make one sandwich so supremely, featuring caramelized onion jam, sausage, egg, asiago cheese, arugula, and harissa mayo, why have other options?

Brad's Bike Shop & The Island Loop

Peaks Island, Maine

Just next door to Baba's Cafe, you'll find Brad's Bike Shop. You can rent a bike here (included with the rental is a helmet and a map). The perimeter of Peaks Island is about four miles, and at a casual pace with time to explore, it will take you about an hour.

The loop offers a glimpse into life on the island. You will make your way through a residential neighborhood filled with endearing homes on Island Avenue, and once you hit Seashore Avenue, your ride will be along the waterfront with twinkling views of the ocean for more than half of the journey.

Peaks Island Land Preserve

Peaks Island, Maine

Peaks Island Land Preserve does a wonderful job protecting the natural areas of this little island. In addition to the usual ocean loop, I made it my mission to visit a handful of the places not usually listed on maps.

The Ice Pond

This is the spot for ice skating in the winter. Although I visited in the summer, I pictured year-round islanders lacing up their skates, piling on layers and continuing a tradition of more than one hundred years.

Parker Wildlife Preserve

An unmarked trailhead along Brackett Avenue will put you on the Indian Trail—eventually connecting to the Brackett Pond Trail—that will guide you through this quiet preserve. These trails are not meticulously groomed, and they are shockingly quiet. I was the only one there, with just a few bird chirps accompanying me from the trees.

Battery Steele

This was the first property protected by the Peaks Island Land Preserve. During World War II, Battery Steele was a critical fortification in Casco Bay as it had a clear view across the North Atlantic, making the island the ideal spot for Casco Bay's defensive system. In 2005, Battery Steele was listed in the National Register of Historic Places. The site is gigantic with large, hollow halls to explore. I'd recommend using the flashlight on your phone, or bringing headgear, as you'll need it to see your way through the enormous structure.

Greenwood Garden

The Greenwood Garden was originally built in 1884 as an open-air roller skating rink. A few years later in 1891, it was turned into the Greenwood Garden Playhouse. Summer stock theater performances were held in this venue until the mid-1950s. The historical landscape, sitting directly on the water, is now used as an event space, hosting weddings, team retreats, lobster bakes, and the occasional play.

Il Leone

Peaks Island, Maine

As you near the end of the Island Loop, as if the universe is listening to your stomach growl, you'll bump into a wood fired, Neapolitan pizzeria smack in the middle of the woods. Il Leone opened in summer 2021, featuring the Aragosta (wood fired Maine lobster, lemon, organic basil, garlic, olive oil, chili flake), the Zucche (wood fired organic Maine zucchini, lemon, ricotta, organic Maine basil, squash blossom, black pepper) and my personal favorite, the Bianca (organic Maine garlic scapes, fior di latte mozzarella, organic basil, olive oil, sea salt.) Fully outdoors, Il Leone is located on a wooded lot that is owned by the Peaks

Island Lions Club with plenty of picnic tables to spread out and enjoy some 'za.

Richard Boyd Gallery

Peaks Island, Maine

An owner-operated, art gallery in the center of the village. The gallery represents artists with a connection to the state of Maine, with works ranging from contemporary abstracts to traditional realism. Open daily during peak season, and weekends in the off-season with more limited hours, the gallery gives you a wonderful feeling as you are surrounded by visual art from creatives who love Maine as much as you do.

Jones Landing

Peaks Island, Maine

One afternoon, once reunited with my mini-equestrian, we strolled into Jones Landing, which sits next to the ferry terminal. Under new ownership as of 2022, what was once a space primarily used for weddings and events is now a restaurant with a fully stocked bar. During the day, ferry passengers can grab lunch from Milly's Skillet, an onsite food truck offering lobster rolls, burgers, and tacos, and a cocktail from the lounge inside. For dinner, the cocktails are still pouring from the bar while Jones Landing begins producing meals from their own kitchen—plates like fried flounder, jerk chicken, and snapper ceviche. We arrived during lunchtime and waited for the ferry to arrive from the waterfront deck—a lemonade in hand for the little lady, a frosé for Momma.

Meet Nancy 3. Hoffman

Peaks Island, Maine
@umbrellacovermuseum

One morning after Horse Island Camp drop-off, I cozied into Baba's to drink an iced coffee and write. I sat staring at the screen, waiting for inspiration to strike, distracted by my favorite game of people watching. A live action guess-who of deciding which customers were recent ferry drop-offs and which folks were fueling up on caffeine before rushing to catch the boat for work in Portland. The espresso bar was bustling this morning, churning out egg sandwiches to people busy on their phones, checking email, reviewing an online map of Peaks before going for a bike ride, or distracting themselves with social media. All together in the hustle and bustle, but lost in their own scrolls.

Chin resting in my hand, I noticed a woman stroll in and head toward the piano sitting alongside the far wall. Without announcement, she danced her hands along the keys. Joyous music filled the space, phones found their way back into pockets, and soft smiles formed among the tourists and the islanders. I made eye contact with everyone in the cafe, each presence acknowledged, and for one song, we all swayed together and forgot what time it was.

The pianist, who is also a singer and accordionist, is the director and curator of the world's only Umbrella Cover Museum, which sits just a block away from the cafe. Nancy 3. Hoffman, who passionately celebrates the mundane, holds the Guinness World Record for having the largest collection of umbrella covers in the world. Nancy, who had her middle name legally changed to 3., has more than two thousand covers proudly hanging from the ceiling and walls in her petite museum. Organized into various categories, exhibits include a nonprofit section, kid-friendly cases, black and white sleeves, coveted designer covers, and even an x-rated nook.

During my couple of weeks on Peaks Island, I popped into the museum, which is open during the summer months, a handful of times. One afternoon, Harper and I received a private tour, while another day I joined a group of visiting musicians for a group tour. In reality, you can't really classify what Nancy presents as a tour because it's actually, in my opinion, more of a mini, one-act show. She'll delight groups with stories of her acquisitions and who donated which treasured sleeve and why, and finally ends each performance with a sing-along of her umbrella cover theme song. Nancy accompanies the singing on the accordion. There are games to be played and prizes to be won, and you happily linger longer than expected in a room decorated with the things you immediately toss when raindrops fall.

Nancy's collection is a reminder that what makes you happy, not what others enjoy, is the thing worth pursuing. You wander into the museum thinking "what in the . . ." and leave pondering which hobbies, dusty collections, or secret fascinations you might be neglecting in your own little world. Perhaps you already have everything you need directly in front of you, and you're just failing to recognize it.

Maine in Nancy's Words

A Favorite Maine Adventure

"I love walking or biking around the shoreline of Peaks Island. I love climbing on the rocks, looking out at the lighthouses. The light always changes, the ocean color and quality always changes, sometimes there are fog or ships and sailboats coming in—I love that about living here. I've lived here for thirty-nine years."

Last Meal on Earth Somewhere in Maine

"It would be at the Cockeyed Gull here on Peaks. I love their food, plus it looks out over Casco Bay and Portland harbor—it's beautiful to watch sunsets from there. I really like their Korean vegetable pancake."

A Person in Maine You Admire

"Richard D'Abate. He was the director of the Maine Historical Society and before that the associate director of the Maine Humanities Council. He is a really good administrator, he cares about the arts and culture in Maine and has at a lot of times, behind the scenes, instigated wonderful projects for Maine culture."

Why You Call Maine Home

"I love islands and when I found this one on January 22, 1983, I remember the exact date, I said that's it, I'll take it. The community here is supportive, strong, slightly eccentric, and artistic."

Tinder Hearth

Brooksville, Maine

Auditioning is a special kind of torture. I could never stop myself from immediately jumping to Step 3 following an initial audition—dreaming about the role, the potential cast mates I'd inevitably come to love, and the insatiable craving to be in the unmistakable, impenetrable bubble that is the rehearsal room. I loved the intoxication of losing myself in a character for a few hours every night and having the privilege of dropping my real self off at the stage door. But to get to Step 3, I'd have to first make it to Step 2, the callback, where my longing got infinitely more amplified because it's right there, just at my fingertips—*just don't mess this up.*

And if I didn't get it, after weeks of waiting for an answer or receiving no communication at all, I would crumble. I'd punish myself with negative thoughts and vow to never care about an audition again, only to repeat the cycle over and over. I did a great job of continually reminding my students of their worth, but never allowed my own preaching to sink in.

But the feeling that shocked me most—the pesky one that developed throughout the years, that I tried to never give voice to—was the confounding emotion that raced through me when I *did* book something. It can only be described as terror. Utter dread. *Crap, now I have to actually do this thing.*

This back and forth—the incessant longing followed by either a downward spiral if I didn't book it or instant pushback if I did—was disconcerting and bewildering, not just to me, but to Andrew as well. Once after booking a role, Andrew found me pacing the living room, cursing to myself. He simply asked, "Do you . . . like acting?"

Good question. It wasn't always like this, not in the beginning anyway. But as my business picked up, after Harper was born, and as my availability shrank, acting became the easiest thing to cut out of my life. I basically threw it a goodbye party and then shoved it out the back door. Acting, for whatever reason, became just another stressor—and I didn't have the energy to attempt to unpack why.

But as any actor knows, acting is a love affair, a permanent itch that, even if ignored, eventually needs scratching. And since leaving my job, with all this newfound time on my hands, I began thinking about it again, warily, and feeling a little itchy. But instead of applying cortizone and slinking back to my own personal torture device once again, I needed an actual reckoning instead of a temporary bandage.

My relationship to acting was always clouded by a strong sense of pride discreetly wrapped in anxiety. If I don't book the part, what will *they* think? How can I teach acting, if I am not actually acting? And if I do book a part, and *they* see it, will it be good enough? I'm a professional after all, I teach it for a living—what if my acting is not actually up to par? There was a level of expectation that came with every acting offer—my own intricately designed, insurmountable pressure. There was no chance I would enjoy any part of the process—audition, rehearsal, or production. I sabotaged myself before I even had a chance to memorize any lines. I denied acting's association with enjoyment and, with every ounce of fun squeezed from it, I wanted to avoid it entirely. It was just more work—another chance to worry about what *they* thought.

I always felt like acting was the most interesting thing about me, so choosing to leave it behind meant abandoning the label that drew people to me. When I would tell people I was an actor, their faces would light up, their eyes would widen. They had so many questions. They were fascinated by my courage (little did they know) and by the end of the conversation, after remarking over and over how they could never do it themselves, they were intrigued. My family was proud to invite friends to my shows, and it was endlessly exciting for those who knew me to see me in a commercial. I craved the label, but I knew it had become a façade. And if I couldn't withstand the daily agony like other actors, I probably didn't deserve it anyway.

Every piece of this art form, which once elicited my most vulnerable and authentic moments, now belonged to everyone else. Other people's perceptions, other people's admiration.

Yet, the desire to act started to creep back in. I could feel the faint longing in my chest. Tiny, scratchy welts developed that needed some attention. There are a couple of industry people in my life who, despite my abrupt ghosting from performing, refused (mercifully) to fully let me leave. Occasionally an audition, or an opportunity, would pop up, and although thankful for their continued patience and trust in me—I promptly ignored the offer. But one morning while busy packing for a trip, I opened my email and read an audition notice. Without much deliberation, I grabbed my ring light and quickly filmed an audition. Normally, I would film several takes, and then film some more, then agonize for a while, then finally send what I decided was the least offensively bad take. But with only a small window of time in which to pack, I filmed it in one take, sent it off, and climbed into the car, excited for a new family adventure. It all happened so fast, so uncharacteristically spur of the moment, that I actually forgot about it entirely.

A few days later, we headed to pick up an order from a wood-fired farm bakery, Tinder Hearth, tucked into the small town of Brooksville. During the morning hours from Wednesday through Saturday, you can pick up naturally leavened organic bread or enjoy divine croissants and breakfast goodies from their walk-up bakery. In the evenings, Tuesday to Friday, the gardens on the property are filled with people, feverishly devouring wood-fired pizzas that *Food & Wine* has declared some of the best in the state. During the summer, you'll first have to secure a reservation through their lottery system to snag one of these pizzas, which have built a cult-like following.

Securing an order from Tinder Hearth can require some planning, some sorting of logistics and some rule following to get the items you want, but it ends up just adding to the charm of this bakery hidden in the middle of nowhere.

Our pickup order included an organic and naturally leavened French batard, a sandwich loaf to have for lunch for the week, an almond croissant (twice-baked and filled with almond cream), and a flaky, buttery chocolate croissant. Andrew and I alternated sharing bites of the two croissants, with me lingering extra long with the addicting Almond Croissant, my personal favorite.

A notification popped up on my phone as I wiped away some cream from my chin. "I booked a commercial," I casually said to Andrew, taking the last bite of the epic pastry. He looked over, anxious, anticipating my usual flood of emotion. "It shoots Wednesday if you can handle pick-up and drop-off that day. Would you eat another croissant if they have anything left?"

He nodded, confused at my composure.

I'm going to let you back in, acting—slowly, occasionally. After some much needed separation, I'm going to attempt to do this with joy, on my terms, for fun. But if this relationship starts to feel like work, or if I pursue an opportunity for anyone other than myself, I'm not scared to break up with you. Not a threat, just a promise.

Meet Sarah Pike

Camden, Maine
@topslfarm

While Andrew and I slogged our way through the early days of the pandemic, taking shifts to work while the other handled childcare, doing our absolute best to survive and remain sane like the rest of the world, it quickly felt like the walls were closing in on us. Our house was not built to have two working parents at home, both oscillating in and out of Zoom meetings, while a makeshift homeschool situation happened in the kitchen. With each passing day, as I attempted to talk louder on webinars to drown out the tantrums bleeding in from the room over, I fantasized about more space—perhaps even moving to a bigger house.

In spring 2020, during one of my daily sessions sifting through houses on Zillow, my mouth dropped at a new listing in Portland. I audibly gasped as I flipped through the rooms, each one more detailed, more captivating than the last. Bright, airy spaces, drenched in personality, pops of color, hints of elaborate wallpaper, and nooks aching to be snuggled into. I had to see it in person.

I wandered through the home, imagining post-Covid dinner parties, sleepovers for our daughter's friends, packed family weekends—and more than enough room to take simultaneous work calls without fear of toddler tears interrupting. However, it wasn't the square footage that wooed me. It was the bunk beds built into the walls in the attic, the striking koi fish wallpaper in the pocket bathroom, the thrift shop finds adorning shelves, the color schemes in the bedrooms, and a hanging rattan chair in the bar. As I finally winded my way down the staircase I must have had that look in my eye; I watched my husband gulp knowingly.

I couldn't believe anyone would leave this house. Chatting with the realtor, she pointed to a small sign in the foyer that read "Tops'l Farm." She mentioned that the family who lived there had been spending so much time at their farm in the Midcoast, that it didn't make sense to keep this house anymore. That was the first time I had heard of Tops'l Farm.

That night, over a glass of wine, we sat down to talk frankly about whether or not we truly wanted to make the leap to a bigger house and move—after all, we'd have to leave our favorite neighborhood and our first home in Maine, having only lived in it briefly. Patiently listening to me painstakingly describe every nuance, every tiny detail in the Portland home I had fallen in love with that morning, Andrew finally interrupted me and said: "Do you want to buy that house, or do you want to live in a house decorated by the owner?"

Hmmm.

I did, upon reflection, remember asking the realtor in a frenzy as I spun through the halls if they'd consider selling the house furnished. But now back in our small living room, bookshelves filled with frames of loved ones, walls carefully painted by yours truly, memories already settling deep into the infrastructure, I didn't really want to leave. With some hesitation, we let the dream Portland home go, but not before I intensely studied the Zillow listing so I could attempt to replicate the design choices in my own home. That weekend, in a sweet attempt to quell my longing, Andrew wallpapered our pocket bathroom.

Without Sarah Pike knowing it, she's my biggest inspiration when it comes to interior design and all things cool. Frankly, I just try to copy her. Since shifting my obsession from her Portland home to Tops'l Farm, I'm convinced everything she touches is steeped in charm, curated with a keen eye, and rich in history. Her aesthetic is clean and uncluttered; every junk shop find is celebrated. She has a knack for creating spaces people don't want to leave. Places that instantly feel like home.

Beyond her aesthetic, I feel drawn to Sarah because of her ability to shift and change, fearlessly, for the benefit of herself and her family. Tops'l Farm isn't her first entrepreneurial venture. Previously she found success in her own frozen-food company and, before that, a job in media consulting. I think we are kindred spirits in our inability to sit still—but what I admire most is her tenacity, her confidence to try on different iterations of herself in a full-steam-ahead conviction to assess, adapt, and grow.

Her Portland home was a stepping stone to nudge her along to the Midcoast where she belonged. And if the beautifully rustic, divinely curated Tops'l Farm is her final destination, her last bow—she deserves all of the applause. But I have a feeling that she has even more up her gorgeous—probably thrifted—sleeve.

Maine in Sarah's Words

A Favorite Maine Adventure

"Nothing signifies summer in Maine more for me than a day exploring the Pemaquid Peninsula. Leaving our farm in Waldoboro and heading south to a tucked-away village of Round Pond begins the journey. A few must-stops in addition to the art galleries and antique stores are Granite Hall General Store/ Round Pond Coffee and/or Muscongus Bay Lobster (depending on the time of day) before continuing south through the windy roads towards Pemaquid Beach. After tide-pooling and an afternoon with toes in the sand, it's a hard choice between a cocktail at the Contented Sole in New Harbor or making the trip north to Damariscotta for some oysters and rosé at the Shuck Station. So many good shops to explore as well—Wildings and The Kingfisher and the Queen are two of my favorites!"

Last Meal on Earth Somewhere in Maine

"Food for me is always about the people and the feeling that surrounds the experience—so of course if it was my last meal I would choose to spend this at Tops'l Farm! I am so incredibly proud of the humble and approachable food we create on the farm each week—sourcing from our local farm friends and fisheries, made with love and care and enjoyed in a setting that is beautiful but not precious. Our pop-up dinners each season really celebrate what Maine is all about—community, connection, and delicious eats enjoyed with loved ones. I would die a happy woman with any and all of these options!"

A Person in Maine You Admire

"It's been amazing to see the growth of businesses here in Maine who are focusing on value-added products with wild blueberries and cider apples! My mom lives on a 50-acre blueberry barren and for years the only customers were those from overseas commodity markets. She recently switched to a local producer and it's amazing to watch this ecosystem strengthen. Blue Barren Distillery, Bluet, and RAS wines as well as several amazing cideries are producing wonderful products and supporting the local economy."

Why You Call Maine Home:

"I joke that my parents ruined my life in the mid-80s when they moved our family to rural Maine and began their homesteading journey. Needless to say I didn't embrace farming and our new rural lifestyle and packed my bags as soon as I could! After school and other life adventures, my husband Josh (who was born here in the Western mountains) and I decided to move our family back to the state in 2017, the year we opened Tops'l Farm. We were eager to simplify our life and dig back into our roots. We live in Camden and could not imagine a better spot to raise our kids and reconnect with all that makes Maine so incredibly special."

••

Tops'l Farm

Waldoboro, Maine

The last weekend of summer was upon us. Normally when fall looms and cool nights begin to creep in, I pine for just a few more weeks to squeeze in more time with my girl, pursue a few more adventures, and complete our summer bucket list. Usually, with the start of school approaching, a feeling of missed opportunities would surface, a regret of having not built enough sand castles, and the disappointment that I had read an insufficient number of books. But not this year. Summer, for the first time ever, felt full. I was satisfied to see the warm days fade. I swam more than any summer before—in lakes, waterfalls, hidden ponds, and the chilly Atlantic. Harper and I enjoyed countless beach days all over Maine, spent more time in the woods than the previous few years combined, and ate ice cream from more shops than I care to admit. Grateful wouldn't begin to describe the past few months of being with her free of interruption, free of pressing obligations. I had the best summer of my life; and although she only has a few to compare, I hope she would say the same. So, we were going to end it on a high note.

In years past, I never managed to get a Tops'l Farm visit onto our calendar. Try as I might, lack of babysitters and prior commitments always interfered with their schedule of events. But this summer, the most glorious of all summers, we made it.

Tops'l Farm is an all-inclusive glamping and event venue in Waldoboro. A place where all you need to do is pack a small bag, grab your favorite people, and plan to immerse yourself in nature. The eighty-three-acre, idyllic farm has a year-round calendar of events that caters to both locals and visitors. Think seasonal dinners like sugar shack in the spring (celebrating both maple and mud season in Maine), winter raclette, wild game in the fall, and five-course summer barn dinners. You can spend even more time at Tops'l with one of their overnights (a weekend under the stars in one of their A-frame woodland cabins) or their petite pause getaways (two days on the farm to rest and recharge with yoga, gardening, and more). As soon as it was announced, we snagged a family overnight stay.

Sarah and Josh Pike, owners of Tops'l Farm and the parents of two kids, get it. Summers in Maine are precious; leaving your kids behind for a grown-up only getaway may not only be logistically impossible, but also may bring very real guilt. After all, there are tide pools to explore, woods to roam, and family time in the sun to savor. So these family overnights, knowing you will be surrounded by other families also spending a weekend in the woods, all lending smiles for temper tantrums and a helping hand when needed, are a true gift from the Pikes. You bring the kids, and they'll provide the fun.

On a Friday afternoon, we checked into our woodland cabin, an adorable A-frame, outfitted with two twin beds and a cozy cot for Harper. The cabin featured a balance of rustic, foraged touches (from a thrift-shop-found bedside table to fresh picked ferns in a vase) to some welcomed hygge (the bedding was divine and the rugs soft). The entire back wall of the A-frame is a gigantic, triangular window, which allows the woods and greenery to be your backdrop while you sleep. Additionally, each cabin comes with its own fire pit—encouraging late night s'more roasting and griddled breakfasts.

There's no electricity or heat in the cabins and guests share a communal bathhouse. You get some welcomed touches of glam, but also some cherished fundamentals of camping.

Glamping at Tops'l Farm in Waldoboro, Maine.

We roamed the expansive property before moseying into the barn for a fried chicken dinner. Adults grabbed cocktails from the bar (I opted for a boozy adult slushie) while the kids stayed occupied with crafts at each table. Throughout bites of juicy fried chicken and creamy mac and cheese, the kids eyed each other, waiting for someone to make a move. Without prompting, I watched Harper wipe her hands clean, stand up and approach a family across the barn. Very matter-of-factly, she addressed another girl and her brother, "Want to play?"

By the end of the meal, a kids' table in the center of the barn was formed, with kids joining from every family in attendance—sharing names, sharing jokes, and making memories. The adults, now happily stealing the chance to enjoy drinks in quiet, watched, smiling at fellow parents during a collective makeshift date night. It stayed this way for the entire weekend: kids glued together in a seamless pack. They participated in bingo hosted by the Tops'l team, enjoyed s'mores together after a Saturday night BBQ, ran free in the grass, and endlessly giggled throughout their last free weekend before school started.

The parents took cues from the kids, as we so often do, and forged new temporary friendships. On Saturday, after a day of exploring separately with my own family, we joined everyone around the communal bonfire, enjoying red wine out of coffee mugs. We shared stories of the day's adventures: exploring the Pemaquid Peninsula, taking the Tops'l Farm river walk down to the water, admiring the sheep on the property, and revealing our Midcoast lunch finds. We arrived at Tops'l Farm from all different states, and the chance we would ever see each other again was incredibly slim. This knowledge, an unspoken mutual understanding, allowed our conversation to focus on the here and now. There's no time, or need, to dig deep—why would we anyway when that must be the Milky Way up there? Is that a baby eagle chirping or a baby hawk?

I am not worried about who you are and what you do, I'm just thrilled to be enjoying your company today. Tomorrow I will go back to being me, you'll be you, but today we have this.

Back at home a few nights later, while Harper tried on new school outfits and began to organize her backpack, we reminisced about our Tops'l weekend. She had already forgotten her bestie's name in the A-frame next to ours, but she didn't forget the fake fishing rod they made together with string or the pretend fish stew they served to the adults. She giggled remembering how she snuck into the communal bathhouse with her fellow girl accomplices, pretending to brush their teeth but sneaking another marshmallow instead. She remembered the secret mission on Saturday night that involved running in and out of every A-frame with every kid on the property, led by a single lantern in the dark, resembling Peter Pan and his lost boys (and girls) in their pajamas.

It was summer's perfect capstone, where memories were formed around the important stuff, on a property where forest, farm, coast, and marshmallows converge.

Wildings

Damariscotta, Maine

In the heart of Damariscotta, in the 1850 Day Block Building on Main Street, is Wildings, a plant and lifestyle boutique. Sarah Pike of Tops'l Farm had recommended it, and if she suggests a store to check out, you should check it out.The natural light soaked room is stocked with unique planters, thriving house plants, candles, large air plants, beautiful books by local authors, gorgeous jewelry, and so much more. As I paced throughout the space, mentally tallying all of the things I would love to scoop up, I felt a sense of calm among the black, white, tan, and pops of green that filled the shelves. There is a clear, deliberate color palette in the space, creating a soothing, inviting vibe. With the soft scent of burning sage in the air, owners Coco and Jesse Martin have successfully created a space that feels like the natural, outside world has come inside for a bit.

I became something of a plant mom. Finally taking the time to propagate my plants from cuttings, something I have always wanted to do, I found such simple joy in watching them grow roots. I've never had a true hobby, so I loved having this little avocation filling the windows of my home. And even though it was a tough choice, I knew I needed to bring home the adorable face vase from Wildings to house one of my new plant friends. A small pop of glee now greets me every morning in my kitchen window.

Lakin's Gorges Cheese at East Forty Farm

Waldoboro, Maine

"I did it, guys," I told Andrew and Harper as we pulled into East Forty Farm, a small family farm producing cheese and farm-raised pork and beef. "We are about to complete my one hundredth adventure." I checked it off my adventure list just as Andrew parked the car.

Well, I completed it. I'm here. I did it. Shoot.

It was only August, many months before the end of my allotted year-long timeframe. Being ahead of schedule would normally be met with elation—so, why did I feel so strange? Andrew and Harper piled out of the car, while I pretended to fiddle with my camera to buy a few more solo moments with my thoughts.

I feel like I'm just getting started. At the beginning of the year, when I would mention to someone that I was completing something I was calling one-hundred adventures in Maine, I was often met with "Just Maine? Nowhere else?" And the answer was always an emphatic yes, just Maine. I could do this journey a thousand times over and still feel like I was just scratching the surface of the Pine Tree State. I have everything I could ever dream of inside my own state's borders, and it feels really good to fully appreciate that. And I really don't want to stop.

But at the core of what was tripping me up, more than my desire to keep going, has been my inability to tie this up in a neat bow, a way to signify my journey's completion in a ceremonious fashion. Having something to show for it, a lesson I can bestow upon people. I've hit one hundred adventures, and the fear and question that had quietly circled me throughout these past few months was still there: What now? Who will you be? You've completed the mission, now spit out what you've learned and commit to your next steps that you have, undoubtedly, figured out by now. What do you do?

But I don't have my next steps painstakingly mapped out. Putting these adventures down on paper, telling stories of my community, attempting to reach every inch of Maine is what

I am doing *right now*. And maybe, once I've finished writing about this journey, I'll continue to audition and film commercials, after all it's finally fun again and the paychecks don't hurt. Maybe I'll act in a play. I'll gleefully write about my beloved state when inspiration or opportunity strikes. I'll consult and teach if asked to, in order to use that part of my brain every once in a while. I'll say yes, and no. I'll hodgepodge. I'll keep working on my patience. I won't avoid "What do you do?" because I now know providing a job title isn't actually answering the question. And I'll do these things before school pickup at three when I have a carpool to attend to.

I'll be a combination of so many things, unapologetically, without explanation or label. I'll do so without sticking an arbitrary number on when I think I should complete a goal or learn a lesson. And with this simple permission—along with a commitment to keep adventuring all the way through to the end of the year, despite already hitting the one-hundred mark—I hopped out of the car to purchase some award-winning cheese.

Lakin's Gorges Cheese (a part of East Forty Farm), founded in 2011, crafts original recipe fresh and aged cow's milk cheese. With cheese names like fresh basket ricotta, prix de Diane, opus 42, and cascadilla bleu—you know you are about to indulge in something deliriously delicious. But I came for founder Allison Lakin's gold medal beauty—the rockweed. Introduced to the lineup in 2019, it has a ribbon of powdered seaweed in the center, and, in 2022, it took home the gold medal at the World Championship Cheese Contest in the Soft Ripened Cheese category.

Allison greeted us outside and announced she only had one wheel of the rockweed left—it had been a busy day and she was mostly cleared out. We snagged the last of the soft-ripened delicacy along with a few of her other recommendations. Eyeing Harper skipping her way throughout the property, Allison asked her if she would like to meet one of her cows. The next round of eager customers were bound to be here any second, but Allison didn't seem concerned as she happily entertained our tiny adventurer.

Later that night, we enjoyed some of the rockweed, spread across some crumbly bread, outside by a roaring fire. The briny cheese tastes like Maine, with each bite feeling familiar in a way. It's entirely unique, something I've never tasted before. But somehow, it feels identifiable, comfortable to me. The type of cheese that once created, I imagine as a cheesemaker, feels like the ultimate victory.

But even with a gold medal, as I am sure Allison knows, you've got to keep going. There's more out there.

IN FLANNEL

5 Lakes Lodge

Millinocket, Maine

A woman continued to beckon me, gesturing over and over with her hands to come to the dance floor, unwilling to take no for an answer. We maintained eye contact as she shimmied and twirled in her ornate, detailed sweater that was perfectly flashy for a girls' night out on the town. Surrounded by her closest gal pals, sharing their second round of drinks, they boogied in a circle singing every word to "Pretty Woman." The talent for the night, an older gentleman with a warm grin and a trusty keyboard, was overjoyed to have his favorite pair of groupies at the center table in the Loose Moose Bar and Grille. The seven seventy to eighty-year-old Millinocket ladies were tearing up the dance floor and it was time I joined them.

I took a sip of wine and entered the circle. The ladies cheered as I swayed from side to side, getting in the groove of "Shake, Rattle, and Roll." We found a rhythm together, each contributing new dance moves for the others to emulate. Occasionally I'd look over my shoulder to find Andrew where I left him, smiling and clapping to the music, while sipping a cold beer. At the end of the song, I stuffed money into the tip jar and hugged each lady, thanking them for the invite to dance.

It was our first long weekend getaway without Harper in about a year. We had arrived in Millinocket only an hour or so earlier on a perfect September evening and quickly dropped our bags at 5 Lakes Lodge before heading out to find dinner. We planned to do a hefty amount of hiking during our weekend away, but considering it was our one child-free escape for the year, I also wanted to offset tired legs at the end of each day with a comfortable bed inside equally comfortable lodging. We'd save camping and roughing it for next time.

5 Lakes Lodge sits on South Twin Lake in Millinocket, about thirty minutes from the Togue Pond Gatehouse at Baxter State Park. While I loved that the bed and breakfast offered homemade breakfasts each morning, featured its own private sandy beach, and offered kayaks and canoes free to guests, what originally drew me in were its views of Mount Katahdin. Each room at the lodge—every single room—has inimitable views of the towering, transcendent mountain. Kathadin greets you when you wake up at sunrise and it's the last image you'll see as the sun sets.

The lodge, which has five guest rooms, recently came under new ownership, and while this was our first visit, I couldn't imagine better hosts. Rachel and Brian, one couple out of the new two-couple ownership team, were onsite during our visit and made us feel entirely at home, but they also made sure to give us our space. Brian and Rachel knew guests came to enjoy the abundant experiences in the Katahdin region and were happy to provide comfort and fuel to help round out the adventures. The night before we had reservations to hike in

5 Lakes Lodge in Millinocket, Maine.

Baxter State Park, we let Rachel and Brian know not to expect us at breakfast as we'd be out the door well before the sun came up. The next morning, waiting for us in the mini-fridge, were breakfast sandwiches that Rachel prepared for us to warm up before our long day.

The lodge is impeccably clean, the beds are comfortable, and long days of exploring are soothed by hot showers or luxurious

The view from 5 Lakes Lodge.

soaks in gigantic tubs in each private bathroom. You can hang out with other guests on the beach with a glass of wine, or stay in your room to get some quiet reading done. We did a little bit of both. We happily said “hello” to the familiar faces we saw throughout the day and compared our adventure notes from that day’s journey.

After our first night out, dancing with Millinocket locals in a busy bar, we collapsed into our comfy bed. And as tired parents do, despite our lofty ambitions to stay up late and maybe get wild by watching a movie, we fell soundly asleep by nine. As we drifted off, curled into each other, Andrew whispered, "Good dance moves, babe."

Meet Danielle Woodworth

Millinocket, Maine

Here's the thread of how I was introduced to Danielle—she is my daughter's teacher's fiancé's friend. Got it? The fiancé, a forest ranger, was happy to introduce me to his friend, a person filled to the brim with stories from her time as a backcountry ranger in Baxter State Park, but he didn't have her contact information. Or, perhaps, he didn't want to give it out to a stranger because he's a good friend. Not a problem, I just called the Baxter State Park headquarters as he suggested.

A sweet woman on the other end of the phone listened to my convoluted story as I asked for Danielle's telephone number or email address. She hesitated and said "Could I give her *your* information and she can get back to you when she can?" Yes, definitely the best idea. I left my email and cell number and hoped I'd hear from her. A few days later, an email from Danielle popped into my inbox. From there, we became modern-day pen pals.

Danielle lives off-grid in a cabin on Millinocket Lake. Her family owns the land that once belonged to Frederic Church, a landscape artist from the 1800s, who was fascinated by and loved the natural beauty of Maine. The original cabin still exists on the land, along with smaller cabins that are often rented out for artist workshops. In addition to being wonderfully remote, the lake is pristine and features views of Katahdin in the northwest—a pretty ideal backdrop for an artist, I'd say.

Danielle spends most of her time nestled somewhere deep in the woods. When working at Baxter State Park as a backcountry ranger, which she has done for the past seven summers, you can reach her after an eight-mile hike into the interior of the park. Additionally, she's been a registered Maine guide for eleven years, so you can sometimes find her guiding for the New England Outdoor Center, which offers activities ranging from fishing trips and wildlife tours to snowshoe excursions, cross-country ski lessons, and snowmobile tours. Even cooler, she also guides part-time for the Maine Outdoor Education Program, taking school-aged kids kayaking, snowshoeing, and cross-country skiing. Her goal there is to help kids find a connection to nature and discover outdoor activities that they can enjoy for their entire lifetime.

Needless to say, Danielle has limited access to and little interest in the internet. She receives emails and texts sporadically and "only when the weather is just right" from where she is posted. So getting an email from Danielle, during our limited run of being email pen pals, was just as exciting as the letters you'd get at sleep-away camp, not knowing when, if at all, the next one would appear.

When they arrived, just as my daughter's teacher's fiancé promised, they'd be filled with the types of adventures that would fill a bucket list. All-season journeys through Maine—ones you'll never find in a guidebook, ones even the best camera can't properly capture. Although I've learned trying to read subtext or interpret tone within emails is a fool's errand, what clearly lies under, all around, and within her words is unmistakable bliss. She's found the right concoction and dose for her happiness and has embedded all aspects of her life deeply within it.

It doesn't seem to me that she is searching for anything on her adventures, because, from my perspective, she's already found it. When you eliminate the pursuit, or the chase of happiness, is probably when you'll actually find yourself right there in it. Her words gifted me the notion that, perhaps, contentment might arrive when I finally stop expecting it to.

••

Maine in Danielle's Words

A Favorite Maine Adventure

"My favorite trail is on Katahdin, the North Peaks Trail. I tell a lot of my campers in the park that you have *no* idea how big Katahdin is until you have hiked it! It spans just over two miles of the tableland, but you look across the entire mountain as you hike across towards Hamlin Peak. It's not a heavily traveled trail, and the solitude and vastness is overwhelming. Small history lesson! It was closed for a period of about ten years, when a group of people from the Appalachian Trail Conservancy (ATC) wanted to reroute the Appalachian Trail (AT) through the backcountry and up the North Peaks Trail to the summit of Katahdin, instead of using the Hunt Trail, which is currently the AT on the mountain. Our director at the time said absolutely not and closed the trail. It was taken off of every single map in existence and all signs were taken off the mountain. Park staff stopped maintaining the trail. It was as if it didn't exist! The trail reopened in 2016!"

Last Meal on Earth Somewhere in Maine

"I'm a pretty big pizza lover! I would have to say if I could have one last meal, it would probably be a pizza from Portland Pie Company! You can go to the store and purchase their dough and make it at home, but going to one of their restaurants and having their personally made pizza is different! So good!"

A Person in Maine You Admire

"If there could be one person that I could meet, shake hands with, and sit down to have a conversation with, it would be Percival P. Baxter. Although he is no longer alive, I hold a very high respect for him. Working in Baxter State Park has completely changed my life, and we all owe it to the vision/dream of one man. To think that he had a vision to protect such a large area of the State and make sure it stays wild and free till the end of time is unfathomable. The fact that he purchased parcels of land over a period of about thirty years, with his own money, piece by piece, and donated them to the state of Maine for others to enjoy is so inspiring. It's one of the greatest gifts anyone could give. Baxter wanted to make sure that preservation came before recreation, and it's what makes Baxter Park so special. It's unlike any Park you will ever visit. It's not loaded with trash, barking dogs, hot dog stands, or loud radios. It's something you have to experience for yourself. Where I work in the backcountry, you see things you wouldn't normally see in nature. Like the family of four otters that live by my ranger camp, fishing in the inlet of the pond every evening. Or the cow moose who just had her calf and is bringing him into the pond for the first time to eat. Then there's the harsh reality of nature that's rare to witness—like the large bull moose with a broken front leg, who sleeps in the helipad by the ranger camp each night, because he's too tired to go any further, but feels completely safe in the campground because it's quiet and not overrun. It's here that I feel the happiest and most at peace. In a place that one man decided was worth protecting. I would give anything to pick his brain and learn more about him and what made him decide this was something he needed to do."

Why You Call Maine Home

"I call Maine home because one day you can be up in the mountains, totally alone, taking in fresh air, and the next day you can be on a beach by the ocean in Ogunquit, surrounded by hundreds of people. It offers every recreational opportunity for any type of person. I love the changing of the seasons because it's always something to look forward to. I have chosen to work seasonally for the past fifteen years and chase the seasons each year to soak it all in. In the summer I'm on top of Katahdin, or checking backcountry campsites out at Wassataquoik Lake, in the winter I am all bundled up, sitting on a chairlift, then skiing to work at Sugarloaf. I love lacing up my hiking boots

> and throwing on my pack to hike eight miles into the backcountry of Baxter to work for a week, loading up kayaks to paddle down the Penobscot River with a group of middle-school kids, or putting on some ski boots to teach a ski lesson. Maine has it all!"

....

Chimney Pond Trail

Millinocket, Maine

I've always considered myself an average hiker. When given the choice, I usually opt for the shorter hike with a shorter time commitment, even if it features an intense incline rather than a long, winding, less rigorous (but probably more enjoyable) route. I'll take a succinct workout, with less to savor and less to explore, if it means I can wrap up earlier. I've always assumed my inclination to choose the shorter trail was out of hidden intimidation or underlying fear that I wouldn't be able to summit the longer trail—but over the past year, I've learned that's just not true. Because I can do it.

I've never been especially good at sports, nor have I ever truly invested any energy into a consistent workout, but, all things considered, I am actually very good at hiking. I have stamina, I understand how to take necessary precautions, I pack appropriately, I've looked over the map one billion times, and I've got the gear. I can physically and confidently do it, absolutely—so it's not that.

It's the time.

I've realized this year that it's *always* been about the time. I've unconsciously decided that I don't deserve time in the woods; there are so many other, more important things I should be doing. If I don't accomplish the twenty things on my to-do list for the day, then it's a total loss. So, if I can just get through a hike quickly, diligently, then I've got my workout complete for the day, check—now onto the emails, the laundry, the *list*.

However, during each month this year, upon reflection, I've noticed that I consistently began sprinkling in longer hikes to accompany my usual short workouts. The mileage is extending, the time at each summit longer, and, sometimes, the hike is the only thing I "complete" that day. That's laughable to me now, to think that I didn't consider completing an arduous hike a good enough marker of a successful day.

There was one hike with decent mileage, a solid incline, and an end-of-trail reward that I had long dreamed of lingering at for an unaccounted amount of time. With this kid-free weekend on our hands, Andrew and I were ready to explore Baxter State Park for the first time and tackle the Chimney Pond Trail.

The Chimney Pond Trail, an out-and-back hike coming in at around six and a half miles, is typically rated "moderately challenging" with a steady incline the entire way up. There are a couple of welcome flat breaks to break up the trip, but the trail is mostly covered in rocks, which require hikers to be extra careful with their footing to avoid twisting an ankle. Many hikers consider it their warm-up before carrying on to summit Katahdin on another connecting trail (five out of seven trails that reach the peak are accessed here) and for some, it is indeed their rehearsal before the big show. But I will just say that we didn't pass one person that wasn't dripping in sweat from head to toe.

I wasn't really concerned about the level of difficulty or the estimated roundtrip time; I was steadfastly ignoring my watch. After all, it took a good amount of work to just secure a parking pass at Baxter State Park, and although I am trying to become a less meticulous planner, you do need a certain level of organization to even enter the 209,644-acre park. Reservations, both for campsites and parking, open four months in advance and often fill immediately—especially if your plans include Katahdin. Additionally, day-use visitors must pass through the gatehouse between six and seven on the morning of their reservation or they forfeit their pass for the day. If you are without a reservation, you can attempt to nab one of these forfeited spots by waiting in your car in a first-come, first-served line—but the first car usually arrives by four in the morning. The strict system and rules are for good reason. They limit vehicles to protect natural resources and maintain a wilderness experience. Also, the average round trip time for a Katahdin hike is eight to twelve hours, so it obviously requires an early start.

All of this provides one gigantic, glaring reminder to enjoy the journey, of course. With our hiking shoes laced up and a quick sign-in at the ranger's cabin, we began our climb. We were really cooking when we first started—almost hopping from rock to rock, passing other families, already, out of habit, darting toward the finish line. Luckily, the incline caught up with us and reminded our bodies to slow down.

Then it started to sprinkle a bit. Normally, my instinct to worry would kick in—the trail is going to get slick, I'm going to get drenched, the foggy clouds are going to ruin the views I was looking forward to. But Andrew was with me, we were shrouded in natural beauty, and we had absolutely nowhere to be, so what

Chimney Pond Trail in Millinocket, Maine.

if I couldn't snap the perfect picture at the top? Furthermore, the rain felt glorious against my hot skin. Bring it, rain.

We took all of the detours to devour each and every trail view. We took breaks to munch on trail mix and sneak in a quick smooch. We stopped to poke fun at the various sweat stains developing across our bodies. We chatted with other hikers who were descending after spending days camping at Chimney Pond, tackling every trail they could during their time in Baxter.

As we finally neared the end of the trail, with Chimney Pond coming faintly into view, the rain paused. The sky cleared. All of the clouds disappeared in a dramatic, swooping fashion behind Katahdin. I'm not a spiritual person, but it felt like an acknowledgement, a congratulations of sorts for arriving at the exact time the universe had hoped for us. I covered my mouth in astonishment as we reached the edge of the water.

Crystal-clear Chimney Pond is at the foot of Katahdin and surrounded by towering granite walls around the South Basin. I felt like an ant in the shadow of the mountain, but also, somehow, simultaneously powerful. It's the first time—ever in my life—I had no words, nothing to title or describe the emotion that pulsed through me. Andrew and I fell into a hushed silence as we surveyed the scene.

I felt my eyes well up. I deserve this. I deserve to feel my body uncurl in the woods and feel the welcomed drop in my shoulders. I deserve the crisp deep breaths of clean air, and the time with my husband. I deserve this intangible connection to my planet, and the serenity I find when lost in a forest. I deserve each opportunity to find this type of peace. No matter how long it takes.

Meet Patty Cormier

Farmington, Maine

Harper has mentioned her desire to one day own an ice-cream shop, be a rock singer, and a kindergarten teacher. She also wants to try her hand at being a veterinarian, a park ranger, a ballerina, and a unicorn trainer. When I read to her what Patty Cormier's work day often looks like, she looked me dead in the eye, put down her marker and proclaimed, "I want to be Patty when I grow up."

Me too.

With a state that is eighty-nine percent forested, the highest proportion in the country, Patty is kept on her toes as the director of the Maine State Forest Service. On any given work day, Patty could be in a helicopter with an entomologist monitoring the explosive expansion of native and invasive insect infestations and defoliations or monitoring fire activity. She could be fielding questions from the media, investigating the climate change issues facing our forests, meeting with various forestry stakeholders, or testifying before the legislature. Or, maybe, all of these on the same day.

I owe a chunk of my serenity, the overwhelming wash of optimism that covers me in the woods, to people like Patty. Her work continues to provide me, and countless others, the privilege of unmatched, tranquil exploration.

Our forests are lucky to have Patty as their spokesperson. The ultimate hype woman for all those who are employed by, or enjoy, Maine's forests. And while she doesn't need another title or responsibility, for the sake of my forester in training, she should add role model to the list.

Maine in Patty's Words

A Favorite Maine Adventure

"I have a few favorite adventures, one being hiking the Appalachian Trail for five months, with the person I ended up marrying! There are so many stories within those five months, the amazing people we met along the way, the special hosts who provided support within the towns we stopped in to replenish supplies, the varying mental states it took to survive hiking every day for five months in any kind of weather, but especially during a major drought that particular summer. But my all-time favorite place to go is Baxter State Park. I worked there for two summers out of high school and it truly started me on the path to my natural resources career, and to go full circle and end up as the chair of the Baxter State Park Authority. When you enter the park you truly feel stress wash away, and there is no cell coverage there!"

Last Meal on Earth Somewhere in Maine

"Weirdly enough, I've actually thought about this before. I would start with the spinach artichoke dip at the Homestead Restaurant in Farmington with a nice glass of merlot of course, and then would get a lobster roll at Red's Eats in Wiscasset, with another glass of wine of course, and then a nice big chocolate Giffords shake."

A Person in Maine You Admire

"I've worked in Governor Mills's administration for almost four years now. And my admiration for her keeps growing. She has contributed to our state in ways many people might not see. She is a supporter of the concepts of forestry, and the workers within the sector. It can't be easy as the first woman CEO, but she seems to effortlessly work through the issues in a non-political way. I really respect that, it isn't easy I'm sure, but you wouldn't know it watching her.

"Another woman, closer to the forestry world, is Marcia Mackeague. Marcia was the woodlands manager for Great Northern Paper when I was just starting my career. I was starry eyed to see this woman in the early 1990s being such a leader in forestry, she truly provided me the inspiration to continue on with my forestry learning journey. I'm not sure she even knows that!"

Why You Call Maine Home

"I grew up in Kingfield. My family had camps to rent out to skiers, hunters, etc., and a cross-country ski touring business with 30 miles of trails. The ski touring business was the first of its kind in the area. These were the days when Sugarloaf Mountain worked with the local towns more closely. I was lucky enough to meet so many people from around the world that stayed in our camps, and there was always something to be done. At twelve I could be found under a camp warming frozen pipes, or plowing the driveway. I wasn't allowed to groom the ski trails alone with

> the old one-ski grooming sled because I would always get stuck in the deep snow. My father would wake me up at four in the morning to go fishing in one of the three ponds that were close by, or to go walk in the woods. I didn't know it then, but really he is the one that probably got me going on a natural-resource career path. I went away to college for one year, then came back to finish in Maine. I just couldn't stay away from the rugged, hardworking, independent people in Maine, and all the trees!"

....

Lily Bay State Park

Beaver Cove, Maine

"It's weird being here without her," Andrew said as we watched kids run in and out of the water, squealing. After a long hike, we decided to head to the 925-acre park along the east shore of Moosehead Lake, to spend some carefree hours swimming and laying in the sun. We'd only visited once before with Harper in tow.

It's a memory we couldn't possibly forget. I somehow convinced Andrew, during the summer of 2020, that we should rent a one-bed Airstream for a long weekend to explore the Moosehead Lake region. We were already living totally on top of each other during the height of COVID, so why not continue to do so but on wheels for a weekend? It was the only Airstream available for our trip, but regardless, I secretly dreamed of pajama parties and snuggling in together each night to revisit our adventures from wherever we parked our home that day. In reality, none of us slept a wink because, with three of us in a bed, there were elbows in eyes all night, Andrew's occasional light snoring (which he will deny), and lots of stealing of blankets. During the entire trip, we were sleepless and pretty cranky and it rained for seventy-five percent of the weekend. If you think an Airstream is already tight quarters, try being stuck in one with a soaking wet kid with nowhere to run and release pent-up energy. And nowhere for you to escape. And limited wine on hand.

The entire trip was essentially one of those family adventure movies where everything seems to go wrong and there is derailment at every corner—a classic family trip gone awry. But always at the end of these movies, there are lessons learned, relationships deepened, and chaotic but fond memories formed. The types of memories that, with some distance, and through a pair of thick rose-colored glasses, you couldn't imagine not having.

Like the day we visited Mount Kineo, a towering mountain in the middle of Moosehead Lake that is just under eighteen-hundred-feet high and with a cliff face rising seven-hundred feet above the lake's surface. The weather forecast predicted a steady, hard rainfall the entire day, but we decided to take our chances during a semi-promising rain-free window of two hours and boarded the boat shuttle. It was us and just one pair of brave golfers on the shuttle heading to the course located at the base of the mountain. *They're nuts to be playing today,* I thought, as we made our way to the Bridle Trail for a short climb to the peak of Mount Kineo. Just as we reached the summit, taking in views of Big and Little Spencer Mountains to the northeast as well as the Lily Bay mountains and Moosehead Lake all around us, thunder clapped. Harper screamed. The rain pelted us from every direction as we raced back down the mountain. Soaking wet, we purchased two cans of Heineken and a candy bar from the golf course clubhouse and sheltered there until the next shuttle arrived.

One day we also attempted to visit Lazy Tom Bog in Kokadjo, a spot that locals assured us was "a place that would be hard *not* to see a moose." It is located a short drive down Spencer Bay Road—an unpaved, old dirt logging road—and there is a little bridge over Lazy Tom Creek where you can park and follow a small brush path to the water for prime moose spotting. Harper did her best to suppress her moose-searching wiggles, but her "Is that a moose?!" shrieks combined with her laughter couldn't be contained. After a while and with no sign of the majestic animals, we loaded back into the Airstream. As we buckled Harper in, a photographer perched on the bridge stopped us and said, "Wow! I'm glad you guys got to see that big guy before he scurried off! How fun for your little one!" Turns out, during our failed attempts to keep voices low with our distracted hushing, a moose grazed just a few feet in front of us without Andrew or I catching a glimpse. Harper very well could have seen a moose, but her parents were too busy squelching her squeals to notice.

But our first night in the Airstream, naively buzzing with happy anticipation of what the weekend would hold, we visited Lily Bay just as the sun was beginning to set. We swung the doors open and were greeted by a huge herd of deer scattered throughout the completely empty parking lot. Undeterred by our arrival, they gathered around the lake as the sky started to shift into hues of pink and purple. Harper carefully waded through the deer and started to sprint as she got closer to the water. We trailed behind her as she frolicked on the pebble beach next to exquisite Moosehead Lake. We were able to complete part of the two-mile shoreline trail before darkness crept in, but mostly, Harper alternated between the playground on site and throwing rocks in the water while the fearless deer continued to graze around us.

Still wide awake at three in the morning with a tiny arm spread across my neck and a leg draped on top of Andrew, we agreed, in one way or another, it was sure to be the trip of a lifetime.

Bissell Brothers Three Rivers

Milo, Maine

The Substance Ale from Bissell Brothers is what finally made me a beer convert. Golden, with a frothy white head, the citrus-noted "dank" beer is incredibly easy to drink—I'm not alone in loving their flagship IPA. We are regulars at their busy Portland taproom, but on a recent visit to Piscataquis County, we popped into their Milo location, where the Bissell Brothers, Noah and Peter, are from. Milo is known as Three Rivers, being located at the intersection of the Sebec and Piscataquis River, with Pleasant River also running through the small town.

The taproom and outdoor area are spacious, located in a former snowmobile dealership. There's plenty of room to find a nook to enjoy some brews with friends. It's family-friendly, with delicious food options featuring locally sourced ingredients and prepared by their in-house kitchen. We tried the poutine (savory beef gravy and cheese curds on house fries), the Churchill salad (mixed greens, candied cayenne pecans, pickled red onion, buttermilk biscuit croutons, and honey mustard black pepper vinaigrette), and the crispy boneless chicken (buttermilk-brined chicken strips served with Italian cheddar dipping sauce and veggies).

I won't pass up a substance when it's offered, but I especially enjoyed having one at this location. Not just because of the friendly atmosphere or top-notch food after a day of exploring, but for the knowledge that this second location was a deliberate decision to bring their success back to their town where it all began.

Meet Isaac Crabtree

Monson, Maine

@northwoodsaerial

Scrolling through Instagram, I mostly find a sea of sameness mixed with a flurry of ads. Occasionally, something will catch my eye, stop my scrolling, and actually hold my attention for a moment or two before I begin swiping again. Often, the image that not only captures my gaze but actually entices me to pinch and zoom is one from Isaac Crabtree, an aerial photographer and high-school science teacher. Usually, Isaac's posts appear before I take my first sip of coffee because he is frequently up before the sun. He wakes before four in the morning, hoping to capture the good light that a foggy, misty Maine sunrise can bring. His almost-daily inspirational captures of Maine's North Woods serve as the ultimate adventure fuel for me.

What I look forward to most in Isaac's social posts is the caption that comes with his remarkably layered images. He'll share the backstory, what it took to get the shot, perhaps some history surrounding the location, and maybe some personal reflections. You'll appreciate the time-lapse of the starry night sky even more when you know it took him more than two hours to shoot it.

I love reveling in the memory of a hike I made when the route shows up in Isaac's feed. To think that I was in those same woods, beneath those summits, surrounded by this untouched beauty that I couldn't have started to absorb in the moment. But seeing it through Isaac's shots provides so much more perspective, a greater awareness of how vast, how forested, and how mysterious Maine really is. They give a reminder that the bog you can't see just beyond the trail might have moose wading through it, or that the aurora borealis was visible from the spot you are standing in just the night before.

Even if you feel like you've extensively traversed an area, perhaps even spent a solid year adventuring, Isaac's work is a reminder that there's infinitely more waiting for you.

Maine in Isaac's Words

A Favorite Maine Adventure

"My favorite place in Maine is the Borestone Mountain area. The mountain itself has a well-maintained trail to a summit with 360-degree views of my own personal heaven. I've probably hiked it around two dozen times. There are two trails up to the Audubon visitor center that lies halfway through the hike, on the edge of one of three small mountain ponds. I recommend the road trail, which takes you by the Greenwood Pond Overlook where you get views of both Big and Little Greenwood Ponds. I don't think there is any public access to either of those ponds, but they are some of the best places to get views of Borestone. After the overlook, continue up the road and stop into the visitor center and pay the fee. You then hike around the pond, up a few seemingly endless sets of stone stairs, and eventually out of the woods for some mild boulder scrambling. There are even some iron bars embedded into the rock to lend a hand. This brings you to the false summit where you get your first view of Onawa Pond. Onawa does have a public boat launch and several snowmobile trails around it. Hiking past the false summit brings you to the true summit, where you get fantastic views all the way down to Sebec Lake. If you look carefully towards the end of Onawa you can get a glimpse of the Onawa Trestle, the tallest and longest trestle in Maine, which is still in operation. I think one of the reasons I love this mountain so much is the effort-to-payoff ratio. There might be better views or easier hikes, but the combo of Borestone can't be beat. As it isn't a terribly difficult trail, you might have some steam left over after your hike to check out some of the waterfalls in the area. Tobey Falls is my favorite, but there is also Big Wilson and Little Wilson Falls, as well as Cowyard Falls."

Last Meal on Earth Somewhere in Maine

"I hesitate to mention it here because it is so rarely on the menu, but the barbeque nachos at Spring Creek BBQ in Monson are pretty much unbeatable.

Kim and Mike own and run the barbeque, and the nachos are a team effort. Mike is the pit master and bartender. He smokes the pork shoulder and then chops (rather than pulls) and simmers in a sauce based around their favorite seasoning, 'Slap Your Mama.' It's a classic smokey/sweet/spicy mix that is just as at home in a cup or on a bun but shines brightest in the nachos. While Kim is assembling the nachos, grab a drink from Mike. My go-to is the Gosling's Dark and Stormy (ginger beer and dark rum), but my wife goes with the margarita. The nachos are piled high with all the classic veggies, salsa, sour cream, queso, and, of course, a healthy scoop or three of the BBQ pork. This is a great, if messy, shared appetizer, but you asked about a meal, and this is certainly a big one. It goes down especially well after a Borestone hike."

A Person in Maine You Admire

"My mind immediately went to a couple guys on the Maine YouTube fishing scene. Joe Holland is probably the most popular and focuses on camping and fishing on the ice, largely going silent during the soft water season. His content is high energy and fun but doesn't hide any of the difficulties of fishing in tough conditions.

"Chris Everett, aka the Maine Trout Whisperer, not only produces year-round fishing content, but also runs a tackle company where he makes and sells his own lures. He produces lots of helpful informative content for new fishermen."

Why You Call Maine Home

"Both of my parents are from Maine and, while I was born here, my dad was in the Air Force, so I was mostly raised away. Every summer (and more often when we lived closer) we would pile into the van and head up to Maine, so I always considered it part of who I was. That made the choice of the University of Maine at Orono for college obvious. By the time I graduated college, my dad had retired from the Air Force and my family was all back in Maine. I had moved around enough as a kid, so leaving was never a consideration. I got a job doing what I love in a place that can only be described as magical. I still can't believe how lucky I am."

Borestone Mountain

Guilford, Maine

Borestone Mountain, occupying almost sixteen-hundred acres in Maine's Hundred Mile Wilderness region, is deceptively challenging. When taking into account distance and the terrain, I'd still rate the climb as moderate, but my heart was pumping for the majority of the hike.

As suggested by Issac Crabtree, Andrew and I took the Road Trail (as opposed to the Base Trail, a climb of about a mile through the woods) to the Borestone Mountain Audubon Sanctuary (a visitors center filled with history and a small gift shop), which lies about halfway through the trail. When we began the 1.3-mile walk on the access road, I was a little hesitant

Borestone Mountain in Guilford, Maine.

to continue on our chosen path, thinking it might be too easy with the terrain being a simple dirt road. But the thought vanished as our ascent continued straight up a fairly steep climb to the top. We welcomed the break at the Greenwood Pond Overlook, snapping pictures of the Big and Little Greenwood Ponds twinkling in the sunlight.

When we reached the Borestone Mountain Audubon Sanctuary, we popped in to explore the history of the mountain and to secure a new hat for Andrew. We learned that in the 1900s, Robert T. Moore managed a fox ranch and fish hatchery (stocked full of trout) on the twelve-hundred acres of land he purchased, which included the mountain and three ponds, which he named Sunrise, Midday, and Sunset. In 1909, after hiring Bangor architect Wilfred E. Mansur, Moore built lodges between Midday and Sunset Ponds to entertain family, guests, and business associates. The land was donated after Moore's passing, with the entire property eventually going to Maine Audubon. In addition to the incredible hiking trails available to the public, the lodges (accessible only by boat or a hiking trail), are available to rent from June to October.

With history absorbed, visiting fee paid, and a new Borestone Mountain hat on Andrew's head, we decided to take the Peregrine Trail, a short trail opposite the visitor center that often gets ignored in the shadow of the Summit Trail. But this beauty of a trail, covered in bright green moss and blueberry bushes, winds itself elegantly along the shore of Sunrise Pond, eventually leading to a tall cliff that showcases the three ponds in a row and Borestone's summit in the distance. The Summit Trail will provide these views and much more, but you won't get nearly as close to the ponds as you do on the Peregrine Trail.

It was early fall in Maine, otherwise known as locals' summer, a time when both the black flies and the crowds had cleared. We enjoyed our lunch on the cliff, dreaming about an extended stay in one of the Adirondack-style log lodges dotting the edges of the pond. Spread out across the rocky ledge, we soaked in the views of leaves just beginning to change and breathed in the possibilities of what fall in Maine can bring.

Turner Farm Barn Supper

North Haven, Maine

My sister, six years younger than me, is the most self-sufficient person I have ever known. As the older sister, I always expected, and frankly hoped, that she'd need me, but the opposite has always been true—I need her. She has taken on a gigantic role in Harper's life—being self-proclaimed best friends—and I couldn't possibly tally the number of times that I have, quite literally, cried on her shoulder. I'm messy with my emotions; she's pragmatic and poised. She's a homebody; I'm either lost in the woods or surrounded by a gaggle of raucous friends. Our interests are different; our demeanors are polar opposite.

But the thing my sister will always trust me with, and perhaps the one thing she consistently turns to me for, is a good time. I'm the fun provider, the memory maker. I like to shake up her routine, and nudge her outside of her comfort zone. Even if at first she is hesitant, she'll never say no to an invite from me.

Knowing this night would be her first time away from her new baby—my sweet four-month-old nephew—the invite needed to be a stellar one to convince her to escape for the night.

We boarded the *Equinox*, a bright blue, forty-foot lobster boat out of Rockland for a roundtrip charter to North Haven Island for a Turner Farm barn supper. The boat quickly filled with animated passengers, draped in blankets, ready for the fifty-minute journey across the open sea. I hugged my sister as the boat whipped along, telling anyone who would listen that this was my sister's first night out since becoming a mom.

Once docked at the island, we followed the group through the farm's gardens, passing a chicken coop and rows of vegetables, when a lit barn appeared at the top of the hill. Although quiet, as she mostly is, my sister took out her phone to snap a few pictures, her equivalent of the "OMGs" tumbling out of my mouth. We entered the barn, made a plate from the extravagant cheese spread, and secured a signature cocktail from the bar.

Turner Farm in North Haven, Maine.

And then, the most magnificent night of food, hospitality, and conversation commenced.

We were seated for a family-style supper at long tables under the twinkling barn lights. To my sister's right was a couple celebrating their fortieth wedding anniversary and to my left was a set of young parents, holding hands under the table, out for a much-needed date night. Across from us was an older couple who were self-proclaimed nomads, living on their boat in the summer months, traveling the world, and visiting their grandkids when the weather got chilly. She was a former theater professional, dabbling in both stage management and lighting design, with a resume of impressive gigs that her husband proudly shared despite her hushing. We were surrounded by so much love, both old and new.

On top of the conversation, the wine flowed freely, my glass often filled again without me realizing. The plates kept arriving, seamlessly, laced in and out of our chatter. Polenta cakes with charred eggplant, just-picked juicy tomatoes with charred corn and pickled red onions, and grilled flank steak with roasted turnips filled the mismatched china bowls. By the time dessert arrived, an early apple tarte Tatin, we had exchanged numbers and social-media information with our fellow diners.

A little buzzed, my sister and I began the walk back to the boat. Thinking we had found a shortcut trail, we convinced others to follow us. We ended up in the middle of a thick field, doubled over in laughter as we stumbled to use the flashlights on our phone to find our way back to the cut, well-lit path. My sister confidently led the charge, proving once again that as long as I provide the fun, she'll find the way back home.

French Mountain

Rome, Maine

Give me a simple loop trail that requires no hard decisions on what trail to pursue or in what order. A trail that gives you optimum summit views for minimal effort when you have your kid in tow. It's French Mountain, folks!

A loop of just under a mile with exquisite views of Long Pond, Great Pond, and the village of Belgrade Lakes from the summit. It's a view you'd think would require more effort to reach, which makes me love this little mountain even more as little ones, first-time hikers, or those who can't climb rigorous trail systems are able to achieve a very sweet summit reward. Go in peak foliage season and you'll feel like you are cheating (or just extremely spoiled) taking in the sweeping colors and mountain and lake views all around you.

Palace Diner

Biddeford, Maine

I prefer to visit the Palace Diner alone, on rainy days when my schedule is clear of any commitments and I am sure I can take a nap after. Days when I won't feel bad that I don't go outside, days where I pretend calories don't exist, days when I don't really want to leave my couch. Don't get me wrong, I visit this fifteen-seat diner whenever the opportunity presents itself—but if I had it my way, every time I'd be solo, sitting in the last counter seat, ravenously alternating between polishing off their buttermilk flapjacks and a gigantic fried chicken sandwich with cabbage slaw and jalapeños. I'd get refills of their house blend ("Ladies Invited") coffee, which is made in collaboration with Tandem Coffee Roasters, listen to the locals chatter, and watch the James Beard–nominated chefs in action in the kitchen just a foot or so away.

Take a self-care day and visit this one by yourself—but be sure to order enough for at least two.

Schoodic Peninsula & Raven's Nest

Winter Harbor, Maine

So, you went to Acadia National Park! You hiked the infamous Jordan Pond Loop, you were drenched in sweat on the Beehive Trail, and you forced yourself out of bed to catch the sunrise at Cadillac Mountain. You should feel totally accomplished having traversed a huge chunk of Mount Desert Island.

Not to burst any bubbles—but did you also know that another part of Acadia National Park exists about an hour outside of Mount Desert Island? It's okay, most people don't. In Winter Harbor, there is another 2,266 acres of Acadia National Park at the Schoodic Peninsula to explore. And the minimally developed, seldom-visited area is, in fact, my most treasured part.

Besides having two of my favorite lookout spots (more on that later), I appreciate this adventure because it is truly accessible to all. To experience the six-mile, one-way loop around Schoodic Peninsula, you can walk, bike, or drive. There is a scattering of designated vehicle turnouts to use to park while you explore, more than seven miles of hiking trails and more than eight miles of packed gravel biking trails. If you can't hike or leave the car, you can still experience Maine at its most rugged self—the window views are incomparable.

No matter how you choose to explore the Schoodic Peninsula, I'd suggest a stop at both Raven's Nest and Schoodic Point during your journey. Schoodic Point, located at the southern tip of Schoodic Peninsula, provides breathtaking views of Cadillac Mountain to the west and also provides the thrill of watching intense surf pound against the rocky shoreline.

Raven's Nest—a dramatic notch in the surrounding cliffs showcasing green, unspoiled waters on a small beach—can be accessed by making a pit stop at the third pullout along Schoodic Loop Road. Across the street from parking, you'll find an unmarked trail that will lead you for a very short distance to reach the lookout point. You'll know you have reached it when you gasp and mutter some semblance of "oh my gosh" to yourself.

Sealove Candles

Kennebunk, Maine

The first time I found myself at Sealove Candles, a candle bar and boutique, was during a school-vacation week—and school breaks mean I'm never entirely sure what day it is. Whether it's Thanksgiving break or Christmas break, time seems to blur together, and pie for breakfast, spontaneous naps, and loss of structure and schedules take hold. But after a few days of family time and the sugar intake has plateaued—it's time to get inventive.

The Sealove candle-pouring experience is something that appeals to almost all ages and even the hardest-to-please relatives. You can pop in, pick from over one hundred different fragrances (with the ability to mix together up to three), choose a vessel and receive helpful, encouraging guidance to create your perfect candle. It takes a couple hours to set, so stroll Kennebunk, have lunch, purchase some knickknacks, and voilà, your handmade creation will be ready.

If you are like me, create a sugar cookie scented one to keep your house smelling like the holidays long after they wrap. Luckily, Sealove is open year-round, so you can always restock depending on your mood—or if cabin fever strikes.

Meet John Walsh

Cape Elizabeth, Maine

"What are you working on?" John Walsh asked, catching me mid-rumination. John, the master coffee roaster for Rwanda Bean, has watched me write the majority of this book, although he did not know it until now.

On adventure-free days, I hightail it to the Rwanda Bean at Thompson's Point. It's spacious and bright, the coffee is strong, and I find I usually write the most freely here. I sit at the same spot every time and if someone snags it before I arrive, John and I exchange an amused eye roll—don't they know that's my spot?

John, a coffee guru, is at the center of Rwanda Bean. Literally. He is surrounded by a row of bar seats giving customers a front-row seat for the roasting process. When my brain feels fried, I'll soak in the unmistakable sound of beans filling a bag and inhale wafts of freshly roasted coffee while I chat with John. No quality writing was happening today, so I more than welcomed a distraction.

After graduating from college on the East Coast, John took a road trip across the country, eventually burning through his bank account and settling in Seattle. This happenstance of a destination would be instrumental in John's life—before arriving in that caffeine-driven town, John had never had a sip of coffee. Eventually, after some persuasion, he decided to try it, enjoying his first espresso drink from none other than Starbucks. After what he described as the "most productive day of his life," he was a convert.

John studied and worked tirelessly in the industry, eventually opening two of his own coffee shops before Rwanda Bean hired him as the head of its coffee roasting operations. And although it's not part of his job description, John should also be credited with being in the role of "front of house." He charms patrons and, more often than not, delicately balances the art of giving people space, but also engaging customers in meaningful ways, ultimately turning them into regulars. He's charismatic and kind, an open book, and someone who after only a few minutes, you feel like you've known forever.

In reality, John is actually someone I should have known earlier.

During one chat, we discovered that we lived in the same building in Portland at the exact same time. Not only the same building—but on the same floor, directly across the hall from one another. I was mortified to learn that for the entire year we lived there I never even said "hello."

The reasons that drove us to our respective Commercial Street apartments were different. My family wanted to be in the center of it all after fleeing the suburbs outside Boston, hoping to immerse ourselves right in the thick of it. We welcomed the car horns, crowded Old Port streets, even the last-call bar releases. John moved in following a separation, and despite the boisterous surroundings, he mostly kept to himself as he navigated new rocky terrain. He was sad, and even being among the hoards of people outside, he couldn't shake feeling lonely.

This thought kills me. We could have invited John over for dinner and shared stories over a bottle of wine. We could have made an effort to provide some cheer when he was in need of company, or stopped to just ask how he was in the elevator rides we inevitably took together. We could have shared some of our family's newly minted, permeating happiness. But I was in my own world, in my new digs, blissfully unaware. It took me many years, and a devoted year of soul shredding and searching, to finally say hello to my neighbor.

If I hadn't experienced this past year, I'm reluctant to admit that I likely would have never taken the time to meet John. I'd continue to put my headphones in, refusing to take them out as my own signal of "Do Not Disturb," because there's no time to engage with a stranger. What a waste to spend time talking when I could otherwise be maximizing my uninterrupted hours to work and focus on whatever tasks I deemed essential to complete for the day. I'd proceed with tuning out all noise, blocking any potential new friendships, and ignoring the opportunities for growth all around me.

And while this is a realization I'm not proud of, I'm so thankful to connect with John now, even if he should have been one of the first people I met in Maine. I'm thankful to hear his stories today, share our many similarities with each other, and know that—despite where I once fell short—John will be at the center of my favorite coffee shop, always willing to lend an ear.

....

Maine in John's Words

A Favorite Maine Adventure

"I live in Cape Elizabeth and my favorite trail there is Robinson Woods. There is a section of the trail that I like to take from my house all the way out to the ocean. I can walk it three different ways: a five-mile, eight-mile or ten-mile walk, all ending at a quiet stretch of the ocean without many people. I walk it almost every day.

When I was younger, we would snowmobile in Oquossoc. There was a trail out of Oquossoc that we'd snowmobile that would take us up to the Canadian border. We would ride the trail until we went off-trail, and we would ride along the border, in about thirty feet of cut trees in between Canada and the United States. Nobody else knew about it, it was just us. I still dream about those rides.

On another snowmobiling trip, for New Year's Eve, we went up to The County. It's like a whole other world up there—the snowmobiling there is ridiculously good. The trails are like highways—they groom them, they're perfectly smooth and wide. We got up there around midnight, slept for a few hours, snowmobiled all of New Year's Day, and then loaded up to head back. We drove for twelve hours total, slept for a couple, rode for eight and then came back. It was like a dream almost—I'll never forget it."

Last Meal on Earth Somewhere in Maine

"Street and Company. I would take their tuna steak over any regular steak from anywhere else. The mussels, the bread from Standard Baking, a glass of wine and the tuna steak—just phenomenal."

A Person in Maine You Admire

"Every morning when I would wake up early to head to the coffee shop, before sunrise, I would think: *I can't believe they are already out there. Them* being the fishermen, the lobster men and women. They get up to do their job, regardless of the temperature or time of year. They are the people that truly make this area what it is. Not only for the food they provide, but for being true Mainers. I don't think I could do what they do—they are what it's all about."

Why You Call Maine Home:

"I call Maine home because, every time I leave, I can't wait to come back. I appreciate the honesty of the people here, the beauty of the area, the fantastic food, the ocean and mountains, the simplicity of it all. I feel lucky that I am able to have a job that allows me to live here."

••

Street and Company

Portland, Maine

If I were to answer my own question, "Last Meal on Earth Somewhere in Maine?" my answer would also be Street and Company. Even if I had my pick of meals from anywhere in the world, the linguine with clams in white sauce from Street and Company would still be my choice.

On top of it being my favorite, it's actually the first dish I ever had in Maine. Long before marrying Andrew, long before Harper, my best friend and I spent one New Year's Eve in Portland after randomly selecting the little city. We dined at Street and Company, spent far too long at our table, inhaled the scent of fresh garlic hitting a frying pan, and eyed the fresh fish being prepared in the open kitchen. Located along cobblestone-lined Wharf Street, the restaurant is always bustling, the food consistently excellent, and with thirty years of experience, it maintains an old-school Portland charm. I developed a crush on the garlicky, buttery noodles topped with plump clams on that first visit—and on Maine.

This dish would be my last meal because it's outrageously delicious, but I recognize part of my choice is likely rooted in sentimentality—something that I find drives most people's answers when asked this question.

My husband's last meal on earth would be a peanut butter and jelly sandwich. Obviously he chooses that for nostalgia's sake, but I can't help but press him on this choice, unable to accept it (are you sure?!) because I just can't fathom him going out with a PB&J. But he's never wavered. I ask my brother-in-law this question from time to time because his answer *always* changes—it's usually the last great meal he had, which is just so fitting for him. I can't help but laugh every time he answers. Some people respond with their mom's famous recipe, their order from their favorite takeout spot, or a dish tied to a revered memory. Or a PB&J (insert a slight shaking of my head here).

Every answer fascinates me, every one filled with tiny delicious morsels of information about the person answering. I find these answers so fulfilling, in fact, I've decided that this will be my permanent replacement for my least favorite, ever probing question of "What do you do?" Once we make it past pleasantries, I want to know more about your dad's blueberry pie, a restaurant I haven't caught wind of, that childhood sandwich that never ceases to make you smile.

Wood Fired Sauna at Nurture Through Nature

Denmark, Maine

I'm back.

OK, so, this time there is not a few inches of snow on the ground. The air is not biting; it's actually really lovely out. As much as I'd like to replicate my first experience exactly, giving myself the opportunity for a proper do-over of my first adventure and a full-circle benchmark of growth, that won't be possible. All good, I thought as I climbed out of the car and registered how casually I accepted this.

The trail leading to the sauna looked remarkably different compared to my first visit. The path, without a heavy blanket of snow, was much clearer. I followed the route to the sauna marked by the familiar wooden signs pinned to the trees, still boasting their motivating messages: breathe, notice, smile. Peculiarly, even though they were prominently placed along the walk, I was greeted by a handful of signs that I didn't notice the first time I visited. As I slowly wound my way toward my last adventure, passing THIS IS IT and I AM HOME signs, I decided that I didn't miss them the first time, it was just that I was only meant to see them now.

Just like my first visit, I was greeted promptly at the entrance. It wasn't the same caretaker, but she still possessed the trademark, noteworthy calmness I imagine is essential to all of their employees. "You are welcome to take a dip in our mountain—" before she could attempt to finish, I exploded with a fervent "Yes!" Startled, but maintaining her warm smile, she pointed me in the direction of the brook.

I am getting in that stream this time.

After warming up in the sauna, with my bathing suit on, I practically skipped to the cascading stream. I muttered under my breath some "Don't think about it" and "You can do it" reassurances as I approached the designated first-dip section. I didn't pause as I approached the edge—I walked directly into the brook, quickly submerging my body. I let out a little yelp in the freezing water while my breathing quickened. I did it, I'm doing it! After a numbing fifteen seconds, I hopped out, shivering from head to toe, and did an awkward, soaking wet run back to the steaming sauna.

My body unfurled in the heat. I ladled water over the fiery lava rocks, creating a waft of steam that circled the spacious room. Lit by candlelight, with three windows offering views of the surrounding forest, I laid down and closed my eyes.

When I finally exited the sauna, I felt like myself. With or without the cold-to-hot experience of polar plunge to torrid sauna, or being armed with a year's worth of journeys to reflect on, I was never going to emerge somehow a newly spiritual, divine, fully centered being. That's not me. But what was different this time, what would be there even without the heat-induced release of endorphins, was my complete satisfaction, and elation, in emerging and feeling like *me*. There was a new, fierce, unabashed protection that I felt around myself—an impenetrable shelter that covered me. I'm the only person fit to be the guard of my own worth. I know now all parts of me are worthy of protection and cultivation, of warm welcomes and embraces.

Ultimately, there isn't a profound resolution waiting for me here, no grand finale deserving a standing ovation. And while there have been lessons on patience, enough content to fill entire textbooks on staring down limitations, what I'm most cognizant of is that I don't need a curtain call to end my journey. I don't need to take that bow because I'm not done yet. In fact, I hope I never wrap this up.

On the way back to my car, I took a few moments to rest at each sign.

BREATHE . . .

I inhaled and filled my lungs with not only clean air but also with gratitude for the opportunity to take this year-long breather at a time when I felt utterly depleted. When I exhaled, it was a full, deep acknowledgement of this privilege.

NOTICE . . .

I stood with this sign for a good while. I eventually raised my hand and placed it on the sign, touching the weathered, aged wood. I noticed the whistling of the soft breeze behind me, some scurrying of squirrels to my left. I noticed the heat still wafting off my body, my flushed cheeks. I noticed that I had no idea what time it was. I also noticed that I didn't care.

SMILE . . .

A grin tugged at the corners of my mouth. I thought of the telephone game that ensued this past year with my neighbors, my new friends, my community that not only allowed me to expand my circle significantly, but helped shift something essential inside me.

I began this journey seeking out people by what they do, as if their labels offered me insight into the types of stories they'd tell me or the adventures they'd bestow, inherently pursuing conversations based on job titles. I unknowingly encouraged the notion that I've been desperately trying to shed—that we are only as compelling as the labels we carry. That our worth—our allure—is wrapped up in our profession. Getting proven wrong has been the ultimate recompense.

I've watched shoulders ease when sharing a beloved trail. I've seen smiles deepen when describing a sublime meal, and heard laughter when a memory resurfaces. I have noticed short exhalations after someone shares the nuances of their job, but deep, appreciative breaths when they are talking about Maine. Each conversation slowly unknotting the intricate weave of suffocating badges from my core—it's something for which I will never be able to repay Maine and its people.

Don't get me wrong, I've loved learning about people's professions and their contributions to Maine, but it's not who they *are*. It reminds me of the pillar of improvisation that you are taught in acting school—you should always engage with your scene partner with a "yes, and" approach. Accept what they offer you as truth, and add on to it, don't stop the game. You do your job for a living and you're great at it—and you're simultaneously a wonderful daughter and a trusted friend and a painter and . . . you are worthy of a million "ands."

We are our adventures, our relationships, our community. Our memories, our admirations, our love.

After this book is published, the people I interviewed might switch careers entirely, rendering some of the words I've written about them no longer true. Their stories might change, and they might change.

Gosh, I hope they get the chance to.

ACKNOWLEDGMENTS

I have felt nothing but absolutely wrapped in love by my family, my friends, and my community while I ran around Maine and wrote this book. I owe a tremendous amount of thanks to everyone who directly influenced these pages—but also to the people on the sidelines who never stopped cheering. For those I shared a cup of coffee with, those who took my daughter for a sleepover so I could write, those who listened to my doubts over wine: thank you. It takes a village—and how lucky I am to have found myself within the very best one.

I'm forever grateful to everyone mentioned and interviewed in this book. Thank you for inspiring me and for trusting a stranger with a piece of your story. Endless appreciation to: Laisee Holden, Carla Tracy, Blake Hayes, Sarah Madeira Day, Richard Lee, Claire Guyer, Ryan Wheeler, Devon Wheeler, Lauren Gauthier, Rachel Gloria Adams, Ryan Adams, Karl Thomsen, Olivia Hammond, Nancy 3. Hoffman, Sarah Pike, Danielle Woodworth, Patty Cormier, Isaac Crabtree, John Walsh, Rhett Fox, and Caleb Buck.

Thank you to Islandport Press for taking on this project and publishing this book.

To my daughter, Harper: I hope one day you read this and look back on this year with the same fondness I always will. I couldn't ask for a better adventure buddy. I love you, sweetie.

Thank you to my husband, Andrew, for continuing to pack a bag and hop in the car—despite never knowing where we are headed. Thank you for always encouraging whatever I dream up, for being my sounding board and my best friend. Your belief in me gave me the courage to write this.

Thank you, most of all, to Maine.

ABOUT THE AUTHOR

Chelsea Diehl is a graduate of Emerson College with degrees in acting and theater education. In 2008, she founded My College Audition, a one-on-one college audition coaching company. In 2019, the company was acquired by Acceptd. Occasionally, you can find her acting on the stage or screen. She is also the founder of Gadabout Maine, through which Chelsea chronicles her adventures across Vacationland and features must-do hikes, unforgettable stays, not-to-miss eats, and adventures for all ages. Chelsea has previously written two books about the college audition process. She lives in South Portland, Maine with her husband, Andrew, her daughter, Harper, and rescue pup, Lucy. Follow along with Chelsea's adventures: @gadaboutmaine